ChRistmas OpeN House!

Advent Stories and Devotions for
Families, Small Groups, and Personal Reflection

by L.S. Childe

Christmas Open House!
Advent Stories and Devotions for Families, Small Groups, and
Personal Reflection

by L.S. Childe

Published by 0 to 2200 Productions

© 2017 L.S. Childe

This edition September 2018

for the family within these pages,

the family without,

and the family that has moved on

I am profoundly thankful for and indebted to you all.

Christmas Open House

Introduction

I spent the first half of my childhood in the humble but happy Chicago suburb of Hammond, Indiana and the other half in Nashville, Tennessee. In both of these lovely places, my family took it upon ourselves every year to throw a Christmas Open House for our family, friends, and community.

We did this intending to offer it as our gift to the world – to share our home and goodies with anyone who wanted to be fed and our love with anyone who had it in short supply.

In the end, it may have been the greatest gift we ever gave ourselves.

Cookie-Baking Day

December 1
A Song in the Air

Picture this:

It's the wee hours of a chill December morning, still long before sunrise, and you are a child asleep in your safe, warm bed. You have a pile of blankets pulled up to your chin with your hands and one foot securely tucked beneath (the other foot is peeking out like some kind of plump, pink sentinel, because otherwise you'll get too warm).

In a matching twin bed not six feet away sleeps your little sister, clutching her stuffed koala, Mr. Monkey (don't ask) in one hand and her baseball mitt in the other. She, too, is sound asleep, and would be snoring softly if it weren't for the canvas-skinned goose down pillow into which she has smashed her face.

The room is warm, the dreams are sweet, and all is right with the world.

Suddenly, like the heralding angels' trumpets of old, a joyous but overwhelming cacophony crashes in on your repose, shattering your dreams into shimmering threads which dissipate as they float away from your grasp. In the back of your mind, you recognize the blaring notes of "Oh Come All Ye Faithful," a once enjoyable carol, now an intruder you wish you could banish forever.

You look around, trying to make sense of what has happened and you find that, despite having no memory of moving, you are standing upright at the foot of your own bed. Your sister has not been so lucky. She is crumpled in a heap nearby on the chilly hardwood floor, invisible and trying to escape the blankets that have ensnared her. You bend to remove the covers from her face, and the bleary, betrayed eyes that emerge are a near-exact reflection of your own.

Lovely scene, isn't it? This fun little tradition is how my sister, Mandy and I awoke on Cookie-Baking Day every single year. Cookie-Baking Day was the day Mom baked all of the goodies we would serve at our annual Christmas Open House, and her final step of preparation before assembling the first batch of dough was to put on her all-time favorite holiday record and crank it up to where she could satisfactorily rock out to it. (Not many people can rock out to Bing Crosby Christmas music, but my mom can, and she doesn't care what you or anybody else thinks about it.)

Upon hearing the thumps of our waking, Mom would immediately summon us to come downstairs so we could eat and be out of her way as soon as possible. We'd stumble along in our matching footie pajamas and begrudgingly comply, downing the traditional Cookie-Baking Day breakfast of Christmas Crunch cereal and milk. Thus fueled with sugar and songs, we would exit to change into our Saturday clothes and enjoy whatever diversions we could find until Mom inevitably called us back down to fetch and help.

I know now that Mom did not deliberately set out to frighten us (I'm not sure she even knew we could hear the music from that far away), but that didn't matter in the big picture regardless. Cookie-Baking Day was the foundation of our gift to the world, our way of telling everyone we knew that we loved them and wanted to give them something special. It took a lot of work, a lot of energy, and a lot of love to make it happen. If all that work, love, and energy happened to generate a fair bit of noise, too? Well, that was just a bonus.

Questions for Discussion/Reflection:

1. What's your favorite Christmas song? Your least favorite? (Do you wish that I hadn't asked about your least favorite one because now it's stuck in your head?)

2. Read Luke 2:8-14. How do you think you would have reacted if you'd been among the shepherds when the angels came to announce and celebrate Jesus's birth?

3. Ephesians 5:19 encourages each of us to "make music from your heart to the Lord" (NLT). What does this phrase mean to you? How can you practice it as a part of your Christmas celebrations outside of church services?

Pray For:

Ministry Teams Preparing and Perfecting the Details of Advent Services

Recipe of the Day: Mexican Wedding Cakes

This recipe was the first batch Mom mixed on Cookie-Baking Day to allow for refrigeration before baking. It also happens to be her favorite cookie recipe of all time, but I'm sure that had nothing to do with it.

½ cup powdered sugar
1 cup salted butter, softened
2 teaspoons vanilla
2 cups all-purpose flour
1 cup finely chopped pecans
¾ cup powdered sugar

Preheat oven to 325°F. Cream ½ cup powdered sugar, butter, and vanilla until light and fluffy. Stir in flour and pecans. Scoop or shape dough into 1-inch balls. Place balls on ungreased cookie sheets about 1 inch apart. Bake 12-15 minutes or until set but not brown. Immediately place into a bowl of ¾ cup powdered sugar and roll until coated (it helps to use a fork so as not to singe your fingertips!). Place on a rack to cool completely. If desired, roll or sprinkle with powdered sugar again before serving.

December 2
Road Trip!

Once you've been awakened by a cannon blast of Christmas music, there's no going back to sleep. It was up to my sister and me, therefore, to come up with whatever amusements we could that would keep us out of Mom's way on Cookie-Baking Day. She tried to help by providing a fresh supply of coloring books and crayons and full access to TV, but Saturday morning cartoons ended early in those days and our attention spans tended to be short.

That's why I'm particularly proud of what Mandy and I came up with the year I was eight. In our bedroom, we had a set of double windows beneath which rested a toy kitchenette that we were rapidly outgrowing. In a fit of unparalleled brilliance, we decided to move two chairs directly in front of the windows, and the kitchenette to the space behind us, and voila! We had created our very own fantasy Winnebago.

This vehicle was the stuff of dreams. If they were really made this way, no one would ever live or travel in anything else. Our Winnebago featured front seats so comfortable they put the most luxurious massage chairs (which definitely did not exist at the time) to shame. It also featured a state-of-the-art entertainment center, a soda fountain with every flavor of ice cream you could imagine, and, of course, two SEPARATE bedrooms.

More importantly, we could go anywhere we wanted. Our family did a fair amount of traveling together throughout my childhood and we usually enjoyed our trips, but our resources were limited and therefore so was our range. We had a blast piling into the old station wagon and visiting the hometowns of family members, the city of Chicago, and nearly every historical landmark in the Midwest, but there were so many more places we wanted to see!

On Cookie-Baking Day of 1983, we saw ALL of them. We went to the Grand Canyon, the Redwood Forest, and Alaska, and that was just in the first 20 minutes. We visited Disneyland AND Disneyworld, New York City, Mount Rushmore, and Aunt Cindy's house. I think we even made it to Hawaii somehow.

If Mom called us down to fetch some jars or grind pecans, we called it a rest stop and got right back on the road when the job was done. There was no limit to where we could go, and we stayed in our room for hours without bothering Mom one time. We didn't even fight (a *monumental* achievement for us at that age).

All good things must come to an end, of course, so we did eventually take our leave of this fantasy world and return to the real one – probably for something super mundane like chores or supper or walking the dog.

But can I tell you a little secret? There is a part of me that remains yet and always will be in that glorious Winnebago of dreams with my sister.

Questions for Discussion/Reflection:

1. Does your family travel over the holidays? Where do you go? What would be your dream destination?

2. Read Luke 2:1-5. How do you think Mary and Joseph felt about their trip to Bethlehem?

3. Psalm 139:3 says (about God) that "You see me when I travel and when I rest at home" (NLT). In fact, the

whole Psalm is about how God is always with us. What does that mean to you? How does it affect your feelings about and/or plans for the season?

Pray For:

Travelers

Recipe of the Day: Yule Log Cake Roll

If Mandy and I had a dream Open House the same way we had our dream road trip, we would fill an entire table with these. Because of the time and precision it takes to complete them, Mom was only ever able to make two for Open House – and since everyone else loved them just as much, we were lucky if we even got to scrape the plates!

> 4 eggs
> ¼ + ½ cup sugar
> ½ teaspoon vanilla
> 2/3 cup cake flour
> ¼ cup cocoa powder
> 1 teaspoon baking powder
> ¼ teaspoon salt
> powdered sugar
> 12-ounce carton extra creamy Cool Whip

Preheat oven to 375°F. Sift flour, cocoa, baking powder, and salt together; set aside. Separate eggs. Beat yolks with a fork until thick and lemon-colored; gradually beat in ¼ cup sugar. Add vanilla. Beat egg whites to soft peaks; gradually add ½ cup sugar and beat until stiff peaks form. Fold egg yolks into whites, then gently fold dry ingredients into egg mixture.

Line jelly roll pan with wax paper. Spread batter evenly into lined pan. Bake 7-10 minutes or until done. While it's baking, lightly dust a lint-free kitchen towel with powdered sugar. When cake is done, immediately loosen sides and turn out onto the towel. Starting at a narrow end, roll the cake and towel together all the way across. Allow to cool completely on a rack.

Unroll and spread all of the Cool Whip, then re-roll. Frost or drizzle with thick chocolate glaze or ganache, letting it drip down the sides. Refrigerate until ready to serve. If desired, decorate with frosting and/or candles before serving.

December 3
The Angel of Flick's Tavern

Given the choice of staying out of Mom's way in the house or staying out of Mom's way out of the house, Mandy and I always preferred outside. Outside, we ran a much smaller risk of being summoned for mundane tasks, plus we got to stretch our legs and look at something besides the walls.

One fateful year, Mandy and I donned our approximately 42 layers of outerwear at Mom's behest and set out for the wild, errand-free terrain of the park across the street. Only we must have been super distracted or arguing or something because we ended up wandering diagonally across the park and down a couple of blocks to Kennedy Avenue. To make matters worse, I somehow managed to tumble into a snow drift and got ice all down inside my gloves.

If you've never been a child in the windy, piercing cold of a Midwestern winter, you may not immediately appreciate how dire my predicament had become. In fact, you're probably thinking, "Just scoop the snow out, silly kid. The glove will warm your hand back up in no time."

The problems with this logic are threefold:

1. Hoosiers are thrifty, so my gloves were hand-me-downs from my uncle, who had himself likely received them from someone else. Their age and my unpredictable growth spurts had rendered them fiercely tight and unable to retain much heat.
2. Snow melts. Even the best gloves couldn't protect me once they were wet.
3. Curbside snow is never just snow. It is full of soot, debris, and whatever else gets deposited into it by the scraping of the plows. I couldn't just scoop it out; I had to rub and clean my wrists of the black gunk too,

leaving my young skin exposed to the elements far longer than they should have been.

I was in trouble and I knew it. After several stalwart seconds of trying to solve my problems, I began openly weeping, both worsening my situation and scaring my poor little sister to death.

That's when we met the angel.

We didn't know he was an angel, of course. In his casual yet somehow debonair ensemble of a flannel shirt and well-worn jeans, he looked like just any other guy. It was the timing of his emergence from Flick's Tavern[1] behind us, backlit by colorful lights and accompanied by a welcome whoosh of warm air. Though it was but a bartender who came to our rescue, he might as well have been the archangel Michael himself.

We didn't know his name, but it was a small town and we had seen this man around several times before. When this friendly vision of warmth and protection invited us in from the cold, we accepted gratefully. He helped us onto stools at the bar and even made us hot chocolate. He kept a respectful distance, let us warm up, and discovered through small talk the direction from which we'd so unwisely wandered.

Once we'd dispensed of our frothy treats, our angel bundled himself up and escorted us back to the boundary of the park across from our house. I don't know how long he waited and watched, but when we turned at the corner to wave our thanks, he was gone. We raced home, hung our sopping wet

---

[1] Fun Fact: Author Jean Shepard also grew up in Hammond, Indiana and wrote about his adventures there in a book called *In God We Trust, All Others Pay Cash*, which was later adapted into the classic seasonal movie, *A Christmas Story*. Flick's Tavern here was owned by the Real-Life Flick, best friend to Ralphie and unfortunate triple-dog-dare victim of yore.

layers and the traitorous gloves on the porch, and busied ourselves with a few, suddenly welcome, mundane tasks that Mom had waiting for us.

Questions for Discussion/Reflection:

1. Have you ever been helped by someone you didn't expect? Have you ever been able to help someone else in their time of need?

2. Angels visited people at least six times in the Bible's accounts of Jesus's birth. See if you can find and list all six of them (hint: You only need to look in Matthew and Luke)!

3. Hebrews 13:16 encourages us to "do good and to share with others." What are some ways you are planning to help others by doing good and sharing with them this Christmas season?

Pray For:

People Who Need a Friend

Recipe of the Day: The Actual Best Christmas Roll-Out Cookies

Tip: Never try to cut corners on roll-outs by substituting pre-made commercial cookie doughs; they have too much sugar and won't hold your shapes properly. These are easy to make with few ingredients…and they taste best, too!

> 1 cup (2 sticks) salted butter, softened (but not melted)
> ½ cup powdered sugar
> 1 teaspoon vanilla extract
> 2 ¼ cups flour, sifted
> Your favorite glaze or frosting recipe

Preheat oven to 350°F. Cream butter, powdered sugar, and vanilla until smooth. Add flour a little at a time until thoroughly mixed. Roll dough out on a lightly floured surface to about ¼-inch thickness. Use cookie cutters to cut out desired shapes and place on ungreased cookie sheets about 1" apart. Bake 8-10 minutes or until just barely browned around the bottoms. Cool for 2-3 minutes on cookie sheets, then transfer to a wire rack to cool completely. When cool, decorate as desired. (Note: We always preferred glaze frosting for ours to keep the flavor light and to allow for storage without damaging the decorations.)

December 4
Snow Dog

Mom never wanted a pet. Pets are messy, stinky, and a real encumbrance when you want to do simple things like travel or have guests over or walk to the bathroom in the night without tripping over a warm, furry lump and uttering unintelligible sounds such as "UNNH!" as you topple face-first into the hand-braided rug of the hallway floor.

She got us one anyway, though, never suspecting that one of her favorite holiday memories would be thanks to that sweet mess of a dog, whose name was Mac.

Besides her aversion to pets in general, Mom had additional tension with Mac from the get-go due to his inability to love anything on earth as much as he loved everything that belonged to her. On his first night in the house, Mac chewed up Mom's favorite slippers and dug pits in her houseplants (already barely clinging to life), leaving sprays of dirt all over the floor. We tried to tell her it was because he loved her. She was neither consoled nor fooled.

The Cookie-Baking Day after we got Mac, he was only about eight months old, so he had never seen anything like snow. Our backyard got what equated to mountains of snow for this short-legged Sheltie…and he LOVED it. He bounded immediately into the drifts from our side porch steps and commenced to frolicking with delight.

When it was time to come back inside, Mac was panting heavily but no less enthused. He bid goodbye to his newfound wonderland and sprinted onto the porch. What Mac didn't know – *couldn't* have known at this young age – was about the insidious layer of ice that is always lurking on Indiana porches.

You know the scene in the movie, *Home Alone* where plucky little Kevin takes a hose to the steps of his house in a highly effective defense against burglars? Well, the reason he knew it would work is that this happens *all the time* during Midwestern winters. Natives learn quickly never to approach a set of stairs in the cold without a firm grasp on the handrail and a very specific, carefully learned walk wherein you place your feet at perfect 90-degree angles on the ground and distribute your weight evenly over them. Any variation of the smallest degree will send you airborne in an instant.

As an unseasoned puppy, Mac was running far too fast for safety, but I think his fatal mistake actually came when he made the turn to enter the door. If he'd simply tried to sit down as he began to slide, he might have made it. Instead, he ignored all signals that something was amiss and tried to power through.

As a result, rather than coming to a shaky stop on the precipice of a fall, he slid completely off the porch and on the other side, spinning through the air like canine pizza dough and landing in a snow drift eight feet away.

To his credit, Mac stood up, shook himself off, and walked with as much dignity as a dog can muster back up the steps and successfully in the door. Since that door opened into the kitchen, my mom heard some of our ruckus and asked what happened. Once I could compose myself enough to tell her, Mom did something that surprised me sober. She took off her apron, crouched to Mac's eye level, and gave him a nice, long scratch behind the ears.

All she said to him was, "I've been there many times myself, friend. Good boy."

Questions for Discussion/Reflection:

1. Have you ever fallen down in public? Have you witnessed someone else fall down? How did you handle it?

2. When Mary was going through a hard time, she went to her cousin Elizabeth; as it turned out, Elizabeth was going through a bit of a hard time herself. Read Luke 1:5-45. How do you think these women helped each other?

3. Ecclesiastes 4:9-10 says that two people together are better than one because "If either of them falls down, one can help the other up." Who are the people that help you up? How can you show them your appreciation this season?

Pray For:

Animal Helpers/Pets

Recipe of the Day: Ice Cream Cookies

This is your new favorite go-to cookie for last-minute company and events. Promise.

> 1 cup (2 sticks) salted butter, softened
> 2/3 cup sugar
> 2 eggs
> 2 teaspoons vanilla
> 2 ½ cups flour
> colored decorating sugar or sprinkles

Preheat oven to 375°F. Cream butter and sugar until smooth; add eggs and vanilla and mix well. Add flour gradually until well combined. Drop by tablespoons onto a lightly greased cookie sheet. Cover the closed end of a glass with a damp baking towel and press each cookie gently to flatten it (but not too flat, or cookies will crumble). Add a pinch decorating sugar and/or sprinkles to each cookie. Bake 8-10 minutes or until just beginning to brown on the bottoms. Cool on a wire rack completely before serving.

December 5
Cookie Crumb Death Match

One of the perks of being a cute kid in the house on Cookie-Baking Day was the ever-looming promise that should any cookies be burned or ruined beyond servability, we would be allowed to eat them. Mind you, this did not happen often – most years not at all. Still, the mere possibility was enough to hope for…and oh, how we did!

Mac was a good boy but he had an odd fixation about food. He wouldn't let anyone within three feet of his food bowl, even when he wasn't eating from it or intending to do so anytime soon. He also sat beneath our table faithfully at every meal, despite all our efforts to teach him better manners, and simply *stared* at us in hopes that something would drop his way. Most impressively, he could hear food falling from any part of the house, night or day, and be at the site of the spill in three seconds or less.

One fateful Cookie-Baking Day morning, my poor mother somehow hit her funny bone on the counter while removing a tray of cookies from the oven. She cried out in dismay as the cookie sheet and all its glorious contents sailed through the air. Half a second later, there was a terrible crash as they fell to the ground in fragrant, gooey pieces.

Mandy should have had the advantage. She was, after all, a mere 30 feet away in the living room watching cartoons. Mac, on the other hand, was deeply asleep and firmly ensconced in his favorite burrow (my mom's house coat and special hair towel) on the other side of the basement floor. And yet.

A mere instant after the crash, Mandy came tearing around the dividing wall. She was only just in time to see Mac, who had somehow already ascended the steps and surveyed the situation. I didn't actually get to see this part myself, but Mom swears that time stood still as Mac and Mandy locked eyes in a high-noon stand-off. Realizing the fleeting nature of this opportunity, they simultaneously lunged and skidded across the floor toward the bedraggled confectionery casualties awaiting them there.

Now, I'm all about some fresh-from-the-oven cookies, but they need at least a minute or two before they won't burn your tongue, and these hadn't even had 20 seconds. They were probably dusty, too – housecleaning was not a high priority in the days leading up to Cookie-Baking Day. No matter. Nothing could stand between these two and the call of warm, forbidden floor treats.

I'm not sure why Mom and I even tried to stop them. It was only one dozen cookies of what would be hundreds and there was no saving them. Sure, these two might get stomach aches and not a few bruises, but why bother trying to break it up just for that? Yet try we did.

I grabbed Mac by the collar and whichever appendage I could manage to get a hold of, and Mom did pretty much the same with Mandy. In the end, we saved zero cookies and only made both of them mad at us. They did eventually calm down and return to their respective corners, licking their proverbial wounds and crumb mustaches as we swept up what little debris they'd left.

Five minutes later, the scene was back to normal, as though nothing at all had happened. But deep inside, I think Mac and Mandy each harbored a secret scoreboard, and both were sure they'd won.

Questions for Discussion/Reflection:

1. What role has competition played in your life? What are the greatest lengths you would go to in order to win what you want?

2. Read Matthew 19:30. What do you think Jesus meant? Who are "the last" in this world right now? Who are "the first?"

3. Philippians 2:3-4 instructs us to "value others above yourselves, not looking to your own interests but each of you to the interests of the others." How can you value others above yourself in your Christmas celebrations this year?

Pray For:

Bakers, Chefs, and other Food Service Workers

Recipe of the Day: Chocolate-Covered Cherry Cookies

The cookies in this story were actually a very old, very trademarked recipe that I can't print here without getting in trouble. However, I have seen my own children fight just as enthusiastically over these!

    1 ½ cups flour
    ½ cup unsweetened cocoa powder
    ¼ teaspoon baking powder
    ¼ teaspoon baking soda
    ½ cup salted butter, softened
    1 cup sugar
    1 egg, room temperature
    1 ½ teaspoon vanilla extract
    10-ounce jar Maraschino cherries
    1 cup (6-ounce package) semisweet chocolate chips
    ½ cup sweetened condensed milk

Cream butter, sugar, and vanilla until smooth; add egg and mix until fluffy. Sift dry ingredients together and add to creamed mixture gradually. Mix well. Refrigerate for about 30 minutes.

Preheat oven to 350°F. Scoop or shape dough into 1" balls and placed on a greased cookie sheet about 3" apart. Press into the center of each ball with your ring finger to create wells for the cherries.

Drain the cherries and set aside the liquid. Place one cherry in the center of each dough ball. In a small saucepan or double boiler, combine chocolate chips and sweetened condensed milk over low heat until chocolate is melted; stir in 4 teaspoons of the cherry juice and mix well. Spoon about 1 teaspoon of chocolate over each cookie to cover the cherry completely (but try not to let it overflow onto the pan). Bake for about 10 minutes or until cookie is set. Cool completely before serving.

December 6
The Porch Cookie Test

In the 1960s, psychologists developed an experiment called the Marshmallow Test. In it, children are invited to sit in a room by themselves for several minutes with a plated marshmallow on the table nearby. They are promised that they are welcome to eat the marshmallow if they want, but if they can wait until their adult comes back instead, they will get an extra marshmallow to enjoy as well. Then the adult leaves and the child is alone with the marshmallow and a hidden camera.

Most of the children sit there in visible agony trying to wait. They squirm, they groan, they touch it and pick at it and even take little nibbles they hope no one will see. One girl (and I absolutely admire her bald honesty) just flat out eats the first marshmallow; she makes her choice and has no regrets. When the adults return, the relief the children feel as they devour their rewards is palpable even to the outside viewers.

Intentionally or otherwise, my mom performed this test on my sister and me for at least 15 years in the days between Cookie-Baking Day and the Christmas Open House. You see, as the cookies were completed, Mom stored and lined them up on a table in a cool, dark corner of our enclosed front porch. By the end of the day, the landscape of cookie jars, Tupperware, storage bags, and stack packs had grown into a Willy Wonka-esque landscape of delights.

Then, at the end of Cookie-Baking Day, Mom always took us to the porch and presented us with the same speech: "These cookies are for the Open House, kids. They are not for family eating. Once the Open House is over, you may have as many as you like. Until then, if I see so much as one missing cookie from these containers – and believe me, I WILL know – I will find out who did it and you will get NO cookies at the end of Open House at all. You'll just have to watch as everyone else enjoys them."

Oh, and did I mention that we had to pass Cookie Land every time we walked out of the house? And again after school…when Mom wasn't even home?!

I wish I could tell you that we passed the Porch Cookie Test with flying colors every year. I'd prefer not to remember the one or two times when I had to help put away cookies at the end of Open House without getting to eat any. I'd rather remember myself as a mature, strong-willed youth of perfect character, but that's just not how people are.

On the other hand, there was also more than one occasion when Mom forgave us and let us have cookies even though we had made the bad choice. I think she knew that some days and years are harder than others, that she could tell the difference between our having a bad time versus our just being ornery. She loved us so much that she couldn't help but to give us grace for our mistakes.

Passing the Porch Cookie Test was a show of strength and will power and undoubtedly built our character. Not passing it was a test of Mom's ability to model love and grace…and she never failed.

Questions for Discussion/Reflection:

1. What do you think you would do in a Marshmallow Test situation? Would you wait for the second treat or just go ahead and eat the first one?

2. The Bible has a lot to say about God's grace. Read John 1:14. What do you think "the Word made flesh" means? How is God full of both grace and truth?

3. Colossians 3:13 tells us to "Forgive as the Lord forgave you." When might it be difficult to forgive someone? Are there people in your life you need to forgive this Christmas?

Pray For:

Those Struggling with Forgiveness

Recipe of the Day: Lemon Bars
Anytime I might have failed the Porch Cookie Test, it was always for these cookies.

Preheat oven to 350°F.

Crust: ½ cup salted butter, softened
      ¼ cup sugar
      1 ½ cups flour

Mix well and press into the bottom and ½″ up the sides of an 8-inch or 9-inch square glass pan. Bake 5 minutes or until no longer soft in the center (don't over-brown!).

Filling: 2 eggs
            ¾ cup sugar
            3 tablespoons lemon juice
            2 tablespoons flour
            ¼ tablespoon baking powder

Combine all ingredients and beat with an electric mixer until well blended, about 2 minutes. Pour into crust and bake until set (a light crust will form over the top). Cool completely before cutting into bars.

December 7
Never-Too-Late Arrivals

Despite all of the work and the fuss and the inevitably sore feet, my family was always a little sad to see the Christmas Open House end. To make its passing easier, we developed a sort of routine for closing down the operations. When the last guest had left (not including Aunt Connie; Aunt Connie was my mom's best friend and had long ago surpassed guest status), we all had assigned tasks to perform.

Mandy and I would blow out all the candles. Mom would pour any leftover punch into a pitcher while Aunt Connie poured cups of coffee for the two of them before shutting down the machine (it was a 40-cup stainless steel urn, so it took some time to cool off). Finally, Mandy and I could pile our plates with as many leftovers as we wanted before we all gathered to put our feet up and discuss the goings-on of the day. It was a lovely, meaningful ritual to us, and it took the edge off of the post-adrenaline blues.

Imagine our surprise one year when, well into the feet-up portion of this process, my mom received a phone call from her Sunday evening small group asking if they could come over. They had kept their usual meeting time because it would be their last until January, but they still wanted to swing by, if that was okay.

We couldn't hear the other end of the conversation, but we knew something was up from the way my mom's eyes got bigger and bigger as she listened. Mom was the consummate hostess, however, so her reply was something like, "Of course! It's never too late to share cookies with friends!" Then she hung up and we all began scrambling to reset the magic.

I'm not sure what job Mom gave to Mandy (she may have just left her to run around in panicky circles), but my job was relighting all those dozens of candles. This was before the days of lighter wands, too, so I had to do it all with flimsy little matchbooks. By the time I was finished, Mom had already restocked the tableware, restarted the coffee machine, and refilled the trays of food. The room was picture perfect. Even her hair and make-up were fresh and flawless.

When our friends arrived scant minutes later, my mother received them as though they were the only guests we had ever intended or hoped to see. As about 15 people filed in from the cold, my sister and I dutifully received their coats and their kisses while Aunt Connie directed them toward the table and Mom served them drinks. The coffee and punch flowed, the laughter and frivolity rose, and we commenced round two of visitation – which might even have surpassed all four original hours combined.

Our friends never suspected they were late to the party – had missed it, really! – and Mom would have been devastated if they did. She is a woman of radical hospitality and would never want anyone to think they weren't welcome or wanted. No matter what she's doing or how she's feeling, everyone in my family knows we can drop in on my mom and she will be genuinely happy to receive us.

Most likely she will somehow, impossibly, already have coffee and treats waiting for us.

Questions for Discussion/Reflection:

1. How do you prefer to practice hospitality? Are you more of a planner or more of a spontaneous person?

2. Hospitality is at the heart of Jesus's birth story. Read Luke 2:7. Do you think the people of Bethlehem would

have found a way to receive Mary and Joseph if they'd known Who her Baby was going to be?

3. 1 Peter 4:9 tells us to "Offer hospitality to one another without grumbling." Why might you be tempted to grumble about hospitality at Christmas? How can you prepare your heart to avoid grumbling?

Pray For:

People in the Hotel/Hospitality Industry

Recipe of the Day: Molasses Cookies
This recipe was a late addition to the Christmas Open House, entering our tradition in my teen years and indispensable ever since.

> ¾ cup + 1 tablespoon salted butter, softened
> 1 cup sugar
> ¼ cup molasses
> 1 egg, lightly beaten
> 1 teaspoon ground cinnamon
> ½ teaspoon ground cloves
> ½ teaspoon ground ginger
> ½ teaspoon baking soda
> 1 ¾ cups flour

Preheat oven to 350°F. Combine butter, molasses, and egg; add sugar and mix well. Sift dry ingredients together and add to creamed mixture; stir until thoroughly blended. Drop by rounded tablespoon or 2" scoop onto ungreased cookie sheets about 3" apart. Bake for 8-10 minutes or until just barely dry on top. Cool for 3-5 minutes on cookie sheets, then transfer to a wire rack to cool completely.

December 8
The List

As with so many children growing up in America, Santa's list always held a certain place of reverence for me, and I've seen it go through many iterations in my years of gleeful pop culture consumption. Most commonly it appears as a long parchment scroll, but I've also seen it depicted as a database, sticky notes, and even a thumb drive. In the movie, *The Santa Clause*, it's printed on sheets of paper that fill literally thousands of FedEx boxes. Santa's list is no joke.

Yet Santa's list, in all its splendor and glory, can't hold a candle to The List my mom curated every year for Cookie-Baking Day.

This document was so great, it didn't need any other descriptors in its name; we always just called it *The List*. In any conversation, at any time of year, if you mentioned The List, we all knew you were talking about the Cookie-Baking Day ingredients list.

The List contained every single ingredient for all of the Open House recipes including 25 types of cookies, four breads, three cakes, 3-5 savory snacks, two candies, and three beverages. It required precise calculations on how much of each item would be needed and what that amounted to in the various forms of packing each ingredient took. In these days of smart technology and an app for every occasion that may not seem like such a big deal, but for the first several Open Houses I can remember, Mom created The List entirely by hand. Even worse, she created tables for them on a word processor for a few years! (I would have run screaming into the void.)

As purveyor of The List, Mom was the Queen of Open House, which in retrospect was perfectly fair. She did most of the work and all of the cooking and buying, so she decided what to serve and how much of it. This is why a few of my humble ideas (licorice whip cookies, Pop Rocks in the punch, a two-foot-tall gingerbread house centerpiece…you get it) didn't make The List.

I will never forget the first year I was officially invited to help with Cookie-Baking Day. I had begun flexing my muscles in the kitchen and had established sufficient ability to avoid burning and dropping things (much), so I was offered the job of cook. Mom would mix everything, and I would form the cookies and get them in and out of the oven. It was a big honor.

On Labor Day of that year (yep, that's when she started planning these things), Mom asked me to sit with her at the table. I noticed as I entered the room that she had in front of her a legal pad, a pencil (never pen!), and the clipboard where we stored The Lists from the previous 10 years. She figured that, since I would be helping out this year, we would have more flexibility in the schedule, and she wondered if I'd like to help her set the menu and finalize The List.

Not everyone gets a formal invitation to cross the threshold into maturity and become a grownup, but I felt that was mine. In my eyes, my mom was treating me as an adult. She was letting me into the Inner Circle, giving me a voice in a family tradition and therefore in the family itself. I had arrived.

I'm pretty sure I celebrated my newly minted maturity by running off and gloating to my sister as I gave her the world's most exuberant noogie.

Questions for Discussion/Reflection:

1. Have you ever had someone compliment you by letting you do or participate in something new? Have you

ever been the one inviting another person into your inner circle? How were things different after that?

2. Read Luke 1:46-49. This song is about Mary's reaction after God invited her to be the mother of the Messiah. How does it say she felt?

3. 2 Thessalonians 1:3 indicates that as our faith matures, so will our love for each other. How do you think faith in God can help us to love more? How can you grow in showing God's love to others this season?

Pray For:

The Elderly in Your Family and in the World

Recipe of the Day: Jam Tartlets
These were my first official contribution to The List. They stayed.

1 cup (2 sticks) salted butter, softened
1/3 cup powdered sugar
1 teaspoon vanilla
2 cups flour
½ cup chopped almonds
apricot jam

Preheat oven to 325°F. Cream butter and powdered sugar; add flour and vanilla and mix well. Roll or scoop dough into 1" balls and place 2" apart on a lightly greased cookie sheet. Press the center of each ball with your ring finger or pinky. Fill cookies with jam in the center (do not overfill, or the jam will bubble over when hot and stick to the pan). Bake for about 8 minutes or until just beginning to brown on the bottoms. Cool completely on a wire rack before serving.

Lessons Mom Taught Me
(or tried to, anyway)

December 9
Hot Chocolate is Good, but Hot Cocoa is Love

As children of a single mom before divorce became the norm, my sister and I were pioneers in many avenues of American culture. We were first in our school to take home family letters that read, "Dear Mom ~~and Dad~~," as well as the reason our pastor rewrote his Father's and Mother's Day sermons for the first time in 20 years. We were also the first in our neighborhood to bear the label of Latchkey Kids.

For a short time there, the Talking Heads of the media bemoaned latchkey kids as a symbol of America's disintegrating family structure, but I heartily disagree. Coming home on our own each day had some significant perks. We learned personal safety and responsibility at an early age, developed awareness of our surroundings, and felt more of a sense of ownership in our home than we otherwise would have. Plus, we could fight and play and make as much noise as we wanted, as long as we cleaned up our messes before Mom came home. We built a routine, kept each other safe, and took care of ourselves for a brief period each day. It was pretty great!

Imagine our surprise then, when one bright and bitingly cold day we came home to find the biggest possible surprise of any in the known world: Mom. Okay, I'm exaggerating a little bit, but it felt pretty big at the time. Somehow, through a near-impossible convergence of events, Mom had been able to leave work early and beat us home. Instead of coming home to just the dog and a chilly house, we opened the door and found our mother waiting with outstretched arms and a mischievous smile on her face.

Not one to waste an opportunity for grand gestures, Mom had already changed into what we thought of as her play clothes, raised the thermostat, turned on the Christmas lights early, and made us HOT COCOA.

This was not your typical water-based concoction assembled from dry, artificial mix packets and puny marshmallow shards. This was the real deal, Mom's own recipe made from exotic cocoa powder and actual milk. And you can't just make it and forget it, either; this recipe takes vigilance in the form of continuous stirring up to the moment of serving it to avoid scalding.

Not only had Mom come home early, set the stage for our arrival, and made us this treat, but she also customized it. She knew that I like mine extra creamy and Mandy extra chocolatey, so Mom had already portioned out little ramekins of syrup and half-and-half for us to dispense as desired.

If you thought it couldn't possibly get better than that, just hold on to your toboggan. Mom also had prepared our choice of whipped cream or marshmallows (the big, s'moresy kind!) to pile on top. Mandy dove into the marshmallows, but I always went whipped cream, no contest.

The thing is, Mandy and I liked instant hot chocolate mix just fine. Mom could have taken advantage of her extra minutes at home to put her feet up and read a book, but she chose to invest that time in us. She didn't just want to surprise us and spend time with us; she wanted to lavish us with her love.

We definitely got the message. It was Heaven on earth.

Questions for Discussion/Reflection:

1. Has anyone ever bowled you over with a grand gesture? How did you react? Have you ever made

such a gesture for someone? What was their reaction?

2. Read John 3:16-17. Jesus was God's grand gesture for the world, God's great Gift of love. How have you reacted to this Gift?

3. 1 John 3:1 reminds us of "what great love the Father has lavished on us." How has God lavished love on you? How can you show God your appreciation and love this Christmas?

Pray For:

Latchkey Kids

Recipe of the Day: Mom's Hot Cocoa
If you dare...

> ¼ cup cocoa powder
> ½ cup sugar
> dash salt
> 1/3 cup hot water
> 1 quart milk of your choice
> ¾ teaspoon vanilla

Thoroughly combine the first 3 ingredients in a medium saucepan; add hot water a little at a time, mixing after each addition to form a smooth paste. After all water has been incorporated and the mixture is smooth, bring to a boil over medium heat, stirring constantly. Boil and stir for 2 minutes. Add milk and heat, continuing to stir, but do NOT bring to a boil. Add vanilla. Beat with whisk until foamy. Serve immediately with garnish of your choice.

December 10
Happy Everything to All, and to All a Good Hair Day!

Along with most of our family, my mom is a Christian. She has been an active servant in local churches for more years than she would prefer for me to mention, so let's just say it's been pretty much her whole life. She tends to sit on the conservative side of the pew when it comes to tradition and doctrine, and she actively enjoys apologetics, eschatology, and Bible studies. She is the poster child for "traditional" Christian values.

It comes as a surprise to many people, therefore, to learn that Mom gets REALLY cranky when people try to correct her occasional use of the abbreviation *X-mas*.

If you are somehow unfamiliar with this particular controversy, just know there are lots of people who interpret *X-mas* as an insult to Jesus. They feel that substituting the X for His name is a way of trying to erase God's presence from the Christmas season and make it an entirely secular affair.

To which Mom will say (and please pardon her language here), "Horse feathers!" Here's why:

1. It's not even actually an X. It is an Anglicized version of the Greek letter *Chi* (X χ), which happens to be the first letter of the name *Christ* in Greek. Since Jesus's entire life story (the New Testament) was originally written in Greek, it's perfectly appropriate to recognize and retain Greek roots in our faith.
2. The early Church used the Greek letters *Chi* and *Rho* (P ρ) together as a symbol for Christ so if you think about it, *X-mas* is really just a throwback the old traditions. It's retro!

3. You could also say using X for Christ is like using Ted for Theodore or Beth for Elizabeth or Mom for Mother. It's an abbreviated version of the name that celebrates love and a familiar connection.
4. Christmas is supposed to be about peace and sharing good things with all people. It's pretty much the exact opposite of that to correct someone else's way of celebrating holy days. Jesus's model was to go around loving and hanging out with people, and we're always happiest when we do things His way.

That's why you'll never see Mom get rankled about someone's wishing her "Happy Holidays!" (*"We ARE celebrating more than one holiday,"* she'll say) or singing "Jingle Bells" instead of "O Holy Night" (she knows, like, five harmonies to every Christmas song and will jump right in there with you) or printing seasonal cups with gingerbread people instead of nativity scenes (*"Baby Jesus doesn't exactly scream edible delights at any time of year, now does He?"*).

Mom will, however, get rankled at rudeness. She would always tell us – and still will today – that if all else fails and you find yourself tempted to mouth off or butt into someone else's business, put that tongue to better use by giving the person a compliment instead. Everyone likes to hear that their hair looks good.

Merry X-mas, y'all!

Questions for Discussion/Reflection:

1. What does your name mean? Do you think it's a good representation of who you are? Do you have a nickname? How do you feel about it? Does it have the

same meaning as your birth name?

2. Read John 1:40-42. Why do you think Jesus gave Simon/Peter a new name? If God gave you a new name, what do you hope it would be and why?

3. Romans 12:18 implores us, "If it is possible, as far as it depends on you, live at peace with everyone." What do these words mean to you? How can you be a peacemaker at Christmas and into the coming new year?

Pray For:

People Who Are Different

Recipe of the Day: Oatmeal Scotchies

The cookies are the great unifiers in our repertoire. We have never served them to anyone of any age, gender, race, or faith who didn't come back for seconds.

> 1 cup (2 sticks) salted butter, softened
> ½ cup granulated sugar
> 1 cup packed brown sugar
> 2 large eggs
> 1 teaspoon vanilla extract
> 1 ¼ cups all-purpose flour
> 1 teaspoon baking soda
> 3 cups quick oats
> 11-oz. pkg. butterscotch chips

Preheat the oven to 375°F. Cream butter, sugar, brown sugar, eggs, and vanilla until fluffy. Sift flour and soda together; add to creamed mixture until thoroughly blended. Stir in oats and morsels. Drop by rounded tablespoon or 2" scoop onto ungreased cookie sheets. Bake for 7-8 minutes for chewy cookies or 8-10 for crispy ones. Allow to set on cookie sheets for 2 minutes, then move to wire racks to cool completely.

December 11
Neither Snow nor Rain nor Trauma to the Eye Can Stay the Rites of Christmas

Moms in general are just a different level of people, aren't they? A good mom can – and too often does – perform impossible feats of strength while subsisting on minimal levels of food, sleep, and bathing in service to the greater good/a needy household. I'm not at all suggesting that this is a good thing or should be allowed to go on once noticed, but it is amazing and humbling to observe.

My own mother's superpower of choice seems to have been time-bending: In one week, she could somehow fit 40-50 hours of work, 10-20 hours of sports and musical practices and/or performances, 10 or more hours of volunteering at church, and Heaven only knows how much time refereeing Mandy's and my arguments, all while keeping us fed and occasionally getting some sleep. Her obsession with Christmas, of course, only enhanced these powers.

Every superhero undergoes a test of her abilities, though, and the year that Mandy turned two was Mom's.

Mandy was the cutest toddler in the history of toddlers. She had these beautiful, long, flowing golden curls crowning wide, deep, dark brown eyes, all on top of the same infectious smile and energy that she still bears today. The name Amanda means "beloved" and she certainly is, but from birth she has also been the best at loving other people of anyone I've ever met. Her hugs are and were irresistible…and that's what got Mom in trouble.

On this fateful Christmas Day, we had just finished our breakfast and were preparing to get dressed in some of our new Christmas clothes. This puts the time probably somewhere near 8:00 in the morning – still hours before

Mom's peak wakefulness would kick in, and directly between the crucial tasks of cleaning up from breakfast and beginning the enormous list of preparations needed to pull off Christmas dinner.

It was at this moment that Mandy, in a fit of joy and gratitude for her gifts (or possibly a sugar high from our traditional Christmas breakfast of coffee cakes and leftover cookies), decided that Mom needed a hug. As was her wont, Mandy in no way announced or telegraphed her intentions, she simply ran at Mom with all the force her tiny little legs could muster and arms wide open.

Mom did and does love few things as much as hugs from the young people in her life, but this time she was caught off guard. Her hands were nearly full of items headed for the refrigerator, some fragile and all spillable. When she saw Mandy coming, she only barely had time to shift everything into one arm as she crouched to receive her hug in the other. She somehow succeeded in simultaneously loving on her daughter and saving our breakfast. She did not, however, succeed in fending off Mandy's wildly flailing left hand, the thumb of which landed smack in the middle of Mom's right eye.

I don't remember if Mom cried out or what she said (which is probably for the best), but I do remember she didn't drop either my sister or the food, carefully removing herself from each before clutching at her eye. It was watering fiercely and she had to force the lids open to survey the scratch. A trip to the emergency room was inevitable.

Mom got dressed (including her Christmas jewelry), gathered us up with a bag full of diversions, and drove us safely to the hospital…all with only one good eye, as the other remained firmly closed making her look like a red-haired, seasonal version of Pop-Eye the Sailor.

I was too young to remember the details of that visit to the ER or how long it took. What I do remember is that Mom stayed calm and collected the whole time, even joking with the nurses and thanking them profusely as we left.

I also remember that despite her certain discomfort, her funny eyepatch that we couldn't stop talking about, and every excuse to throw in the towel, Mom didn't miss a single step once we returned home. We had Christmas dinner as usual with all of the pomp, ceremony, and accoutrements that always made it special to our family.

And we had it ON TIME.

Questions for Discussion/Reflection:

1. Have you ever had an injury or illness that interfered with something special happening in your life? What did you do?

2. Read Matthew 1:18-25. Joseph had what must have felt like a setback in his plans to take Mary as his wife. According to these verses, what made him decide to keep moving forward?

3. Interruptions to our plans are inevitable. Some force us to make changes while others give us the opportunity to become stronger by pushing through. In Isaiah 41:13, God says, "I am the LORD your God who takes hold of your right hand and says to you, 'Do not fear; I will help you.'" How does this verse apply to both kinds of setbacks?

Pray For:

Medical Professionals

Recipe of the Day: Thumbprint Cookies

Sorry, Mom.

> 1 cup (2 sticks) salted butter, softened
> 2/3 cup sugar
> 2 eggs, separated
> 1 teaspoon vanilla
> 2 cups flour

Cream butter and sugar; add egg yolks and mix until fluffy. Stir in vanilla and flour; mix well. Chill at least 30 minutes.

Preheat the oven to 350°F. Roll or scoop dough into 2" balls. Dip each ball into slightly beaten egg whites, then place on a cookie sheet at least 2" apart. Bake for 7 minutes, then make a thumbprint in the center of each cookie. Continue baking for 2-3 minutes or until just beginning to brown at the edges. Remove and cool completely. When cookies are cool, fill the thumbprints with the frosting of your choice (we use homemade chocolate buttercream).

December 12
You Don't Have to Choose

In my family, *nerd* is a compliment.

A nerd is anyone who is single-mindedly committed to intellectual pursuits, usually in a specific field. I'm a pop culture nerd, my sister is a music nerd, Mom is a Christmas nerd... You get it. You can be a nerd in more than one thing, of course, and most of us are. The point is that you love something and you are committed to enjoying it and learning as much about it as you can.

Our Christmases, therefore, were naturally full of nerdy pursuits as well, one being our annual pilgrimage to the Adler Planetarium in Chicago for its "Star of Wonder" sky show. They've since retired the show, but it was an entrancing hour-long exploration of the origins of the Star of Bethlehem, and we loved it enough to endure Chicago traffic and literally hours in line every year until we moved away. (Except for Mandy, that is; the sweeping cinematography actually gave her horrible motion sickness. My mom never caught on, though, so Mandy would stoically parade in with the rest of us, grip her armrests, and just try to keep her eyes closed until it was over.)

Here are some of the things that "Star of Wonder" taught me:

- Most researchers agree that Jesus was born between 3 BC and 1 AD. It's always possible that the star was its own unique event, but astronomers can use computer simulations to reproduce the night sky as it was then, and multiple trackable celestial events could have created the star that the Magi referenced to pinpoint Jesus's birth.
- My favorite example is in 2 BC when Venus and Jupiter converged so closely that they would have looked like

one single, brilliant star. This occurred near Regulus in the constellation of Leo, which symbolized royalty and power to the Magi (who were both astronomers and astrologers). At that time, Jupiter was known as the "planet of Kings" and Venus as a symbol of new life.

- Other events took place around this time which could have created the phenomenon, including other planetary movements, comets, and possibly even a supernova.

There's much more to it of course, but here's the most important takeaway for me as a kid: science and faith are friends. Science shows us *how* things work, and faith shows us why/what it all means. They are not in competition; they work together to make us smarter in both!

Leaving the planetarium theater each Christmas season, I experienced renewed enthusiasm for observing the heart and handiwork of God in creation around me, for continuing to learn about how things work and why. It was so encouraging to know I could be both a Bible nerd AND a science nerd! I was energized and affirmed.

Mandy was just seasick.

Questions for Discussion/Reflection:

1. Have you ever been called a nerd? Have you ever considered it a compliment? What is something you love about which people could call you a nerd?

2. Read Matthew 2:1-12. Many scholars believe that the Magi knew how to interpret the star due to the passed-down teachings of Daniel the prophet. So they were star nerds and prophecy nerds! What other prophecies

can you find that were fulfilled by Jesus?

3. Psalm 8:1 says about God, "You have set Your glory in the heavens." What do you think David meant by these words? What do they mean to you?

Pray For:

Scientists and Bible Teachers

Recipe of the Day: 7-Layer Cookie Bars
Because life, learning, and nerdom all have layers!

1 stick salted butter
1 cup graham cracker crumbs
1 cup sweetened shredded coconut
1 cup white chocolate chips
1 cup semi-sweet chocolate chips
14-ounce can sweetened condensed milk
1 cup coarsely chopped pecans

Preheat the oven to 350°F (325°F if using a glass baking dish). Place butter in your pan and the pan in the oven until the butter is melted. Press graham cracker crumbs into the (evenly distributed!) melted butter to fill the bottom of the pan. Layer the chips and coconut evenly over top of the crust. Drizzle the sweetened condensed milk evenly over the entire surface of the mixture, then sprinkle with nuts. Bake for 25-30 minutes, or until the top is barely brown. Let cool completely before cutting into bars.

December 13
Leg Warmers Don't Go on the Outside of Your Pants

Chicago, Illinois is famous for many things. Not only is it the third largest city in the United States, it's also the home of:

- the greatest team of football players ever assembled in the history of the sport (1986's Super Bowl 20 champions, go Bears!)
- the Sears Tower (some may call by its more recent name, the Willis Tower, but I just can't)
- several health food movements centered around hot dogs and pizza cuisine.

Most notorious, however, is Chicago's propensity for winds so strong you'd swear they could pick you up and actually carry you to your destination. In temperate months, such a wind is your friend, supporting your kite-flying habits and keeping you cool as you jog along Lakeshore Drive. You know when they're not your friend? When temperatures are hovering around freezing and your family's annual holiday kick-off tradition is heading into the city for the Christmas Tree Lighting Ceremony on Daley Plaza. Yet that's what we did every Friday after Thanksgiving in my childhood of the early eighties...and we LOVED it.

Mom scheduled the trips around the tree lighting, but for me it was everything leading up to that which really mattered. There were decorations on every lamppost, vendors of hot chocolate and actual roasted chestnuts scattered along the sidewalks, and most important of all, the windows.

Chicago stores at that time converted their window displays into Christmas scenes which they debuted the day after Thanksgiving. These displays always featured animatronic characters and other moving set pieces, and they were magical portals into another world. Mandy's favorite windows were the ones with Santa's workshop; I was always entranced by the Nutcracker story, especially the window that showed Clara saving the Nutcracker by throwing her shoe to distract the Rat King. (That was probably the birth of feminism for me.)

Even the most magical moments, however, can be difficult to enjoy when your legs are falling off from the cold, which was the predicament I found myself in during one of the early years. It was a particularly cold day with higher than average wind speeds, and Mom had done everything she could to help. She provided Mandy and me with weatherproof coats, double layers of hats and gloves and socks, and even had us wear both tights and leg warmers with our pants. We should have been fine.

Except that what Mom had failed to do was supervise the application of all these layers. This was my first time ever wearing leg warmers and since all I had used up to this point was snow pants, I put them on the same way: over my pants. The whole function of leg warmers, I came to learn, is to trap your body heat in underneath another layer; if they're over your pants, they just squeeze everything tight and let out all the heat. Add that to the piercing Chicago wind, and I began to lose feeling in my lower extremities within moments of exiting the car.

I don't know which my mother noticed first, my uncontrollable shivering or the way my jeans were smashed inside my poor, near-to-bursting leg warmers like overfilled woolen sausages, but she whisked me into the nearest public bathroom to set the situation right. And you know, after those adjustments and some hot chocolate to get my body temperature back to normal, I was able to have a lot more fun!

Questions for Discussion/Reflection:

1. Have you ever been stumped by a tool or piece of equipment – used it the wrong way or couldn't get it to work at all? What happened? How did you correct it?

2. Read Luke 1:5-20. Zechariah was given an amazing experience, a one-on-one visit with an archangel to receive a message from the Lord – and he flubbed it. How do you think you would have reacted in his position?

3. Colossians 4:5 encourages us to "make the most of every opportunity," particularly with our words and the way we treat outsiders. How can you make this a priority as you are out and about this season?

Pray For:

People with Disabilities

Recipe of the Day: Gingerbread Nutcrackers
Obviously.

> ¾ cup salted butter, softened
> 1 cup packed brown sugar
> 1 egg
> ¾ cup molasses
> 4 cups all-purpose flour
> 2 teaspoons ground ginger
> 1 ½ teaspoons baking soda
> 1 ½ teaspoons ground cinnamon
> ¾ teaspoon ground cloves
>
> vanilla decorator frosting
> mini gum drops, cinnamon imperials, and/or other
> desired decorations

Cream butter and brown sugar until light and fluffy. Add egg and molasses; mix well. Sift dry ingredients together and add to creamed mixture gradually until thoroughly blended. Cover and refrigerate for 4-12 hours.

Preheat the oven to 350°F. Roll dough out on a lightly floured surface to about ¼-inch thickness. Use cookie cutters to cut out desired shapes and place on ungreased cookie sheets about 1" apart. Bake 8-10 minutes or until just barely dry on top. Cool for 2-3 minutes on cookie sheets, then transfer to a wire rack to cool completely. When cool, decorate as desired.

December 14
You Wear a Jacket on Christmas

The Christmas that I turned seven, I got a bike, which was kind of a risk on my mom's part. A typical winter in Hammond was sure to feature freezing temperatures accompanied by that ever-present Lake Michigan wind and snow drifts of two feet or better. What should have happened was that I would receive the bike with leaps of joy, beg to go out and ride it, and be allowed maybe 5 minutes outside if it was cold, or refused completely if there was snow (so the chain wouldn't rust).

This must have been a divinely appointed bike, however, because when we awoke that Christmas morning, the sun was shining and it was unseasonably warm at a balmy 65 degrees. Once dressed and full to the gills with Christmas breakfast, Mandy (who had herself received a new tricycle) and I shot out of the house as if from a cannon and commenced our epic sidewalk rocket adventures.

That's one thing for which I will always be grateful about the Hammond of my youth: its ubiquitous sidewalks. They weren't always in great repair, but we had a reliable place to walk, run, and now ride our bikes safely away from any errant traffic. We were free to go from stop sign to stop sign on an endless loop with no supervision – as long as we listened and came when Mom called, of course.

My bike was a shiny pink dream with a banana seat, a woven plastic basket on the front, and of course, pink streamers on the handlebars. On it, I instantly became Wonder Woman in her invisible jet, soaring over all the corners of the earth, seeking the distressed to save and injustices to set right. Evil forces (and little sisters), beware!

Suddenly impinging on my scene in the clouds came a voice on the wind calling my name. Reluctant to leave my fantasy world yet fearful of the consequences of ignoring that voice, I glanced over my shoulder. There in the distance, actually chasing me down, was the ardent if winded figure of my mom. In her hand, waving over her head like an emergency flare on a leash, was my good old navy blue windbreaker.

Looking at my sister with her cheeks aglow and freshly bundled in her pink hooded sweater, I knew what was about to happen. I tried to fight it anyway. I turned my bike around as slowly as I could and met my mom halfway home. As she tried to hand me the jacket, I resisted with objections that were lucid, intelligent, and well thought-out. It's warm! It's sunny! I'm actually sweaty already, just look at me!

Mom eyed me levelly as she listened to every word, but all she said in reply was, "It's Christmas, young lady. Put it on."

To this day, I'm not entirely clear on what that statement was meant to impart. It's Christmas…so what? Is wearing a jacket part of some sacred tradition? Was I to put it on just in case of a sudden arctic breeze? Do we somehow honor Baby Jesus with our outerwear?

I don't know and it doesn't really matter. My mom gave me a bike, her endless love, and a super great Christmas every year. There was then and is now no better way to give back than to honor and respect her wishes.

Besides, once I got really going, the way that windbreaker flew out behind me and flapped in the wind…it was almost like a cape.

Questions for Discussion/Reflection:

1. What does the perfect Christmas morning look like to you? Do you prefer a white Christmas or temperate climes, sun or rain, clouds or clear skies?

2. Matthew 1:1-17 gives us a list of Jesus's ancestors beginning with Abraham. Such a list traditionally would feature only the names of the men, but Matthew highlights four women as well. Can you find their names? Why do you think these women were included in Jesus's genealogy?

3. "Honor your father and your mother" is the fifth of the 10 Commandments and found in Exodus 20:12. Look up the Hebrew word used for "honor" in this verse. What does it mean? What does it mean to you, and how can you observe it this season?

Pray For:

Parents

Recipe of the Day: Christmas Wreath Coffee Cake

This unique coffee cake is still the centerpiece of our Christmas breakfasts today (and I'm pretty sure it still gives superpowers).

½ cup warm water
1 package dry yeast
1 egg
2 ½ cups Biquick™
1 tablespoon sugar
½ cup salted butter, melted
1 cup brown sugar
1/3 cup sugar
cinnamon to taste
1 cup chopped pecans or walnuts

white frosting glaze (We use ¾ cup powdered sugar and 1-2 teaspoons of milk.)
red and green decorating sugar and/or gel frosting

Dissolve yeast in water. Add egg, sugar, and Bisquick™; beat for 2 minutes. Knead dough on a surface well-floured with Bisquick™ about 20 times. Roll into a rectangle measuring about 9"x16". Spread with melted butter, then sprinkle generously with brown sugar, sugar, cinnamon, and nuts. Roll tightly from the wide side across, then seal by pinching. Place sealed-side-down in a glass pie pan. Cut with scissors all the way around the circle at 1" intervals, about 2/3 through the depth of the roll, then rotate the roll slightly so the cuts fan out around the edge. Let rise 1 hour. Bake at 375°F for 15-20 minutes or until golden brown (cooked through, but not dried out!). Cool at least 30 minutes before adding glaze and colored sugar. If desired, when completely cool, add a bow, berries, and other accents with decorating gel.

December 15
Snow Days are the Real Deal

Snow days are a phenomenon I never had the privilege to experience until we moved from Indiana to Tennessee – where, in fact, the term is a bit of misnomer. You don't actually have to have snow on the ground to get a Snow Day in Tennessee. In my school career there, we got Snow Days for (I am not making any of these up): snow, ice, the threat of snow or ice, the threat of snow or ice to a nearby county, too much cold, too much wind, and the flu.

No matter what the cause, when the Snow Days were over and it was time to return to school, my friends and I were always tempted to say something like, "Well, back to reality..." But is it, though? Is our normal routine the true definition of reality, or could it be that daily life itself is the illusion? Here's a comparison of regular days vs. Snow Days with my mom to help you see what I mean.

Food – On a regular day, food was what happened between activities and obligations. We'd have whatever we could eat in the car for breakfast and whatever lunch we could inhale within our pitiful 20-minute periods. Mom was good at making sure we ate dinner together, but there was always a limit to the sharing due to homework, activities, and understandable fatigue.

On a Snow Day, food was an act of love. French toast with bacon and strawberries, heaping pots of slow-cooked chili, indoor s'mores and homemade sugar cookies...nothing was too good or too laborious for us. The kitchen was a veritable playground for trying new things and turning nutrition into an art form.

Fun – On a regular day, our focus was mostly on function. That's understandable, because we were busy and with mostly noble pursuits. Maybe we'd sing along with a good song on the radio, tell a funny story over dinner, or catch a fleeting TV show together, and those moments were nice but were hardly ever enough.

On a Snow Day, we could barely function because we were having so much fun! The day was too full of playing in the snow, watching movies, reading comic books (or any books!), finger painting, eating too much, and then going back outside to start it all over again. It was a soggy, beautiful, mad mess all the day long.

Free Time – On a regular day, free time was...wait a minute, free time? What was that?

On a Snow Day, we were given the gift of a mandatory Sabbath. We stopped to look at the sky. We got outside to enjoy and appreciate nature. We took time for the things that energized us and for the people we loved. Our routines were broken, our fallbacks were shaken up, and we only had ourselves and whatever we brought with us into the day. We were at rest (if not well rested).

On a regular day, we did what was necessary.
On a Snow Day, we did what we were made for.

THAT is the real life.

Questions for Discussion/Reflection:

1. Holidays (or "holy days") are meant to be set apart to relax and pay special attention to God's place in our history and our lives. Is this usually your experience? Why or why not?

2. Read Luke 2:19. This was after the shepherds visited and shared their story. What do you think it means that Mary treasured and pondered these things?

3. Exodus 20:8 gives us the fourth of the 10 Commandments, which is to "Remember the Sabbath day to keep it holy." What does the word Sabbath mean to you? How faithful are you at remembering and practicing it? How can you incorporate Sabbath into your Christmas plans this year?

Pray For:

People Who Need a Break

Recipe of the Day: No-Bake Crispy Date Snowballs
Don't actually throw these at someone, though. It will sting!

½ cup salted butter
¾ cup honey
8 ounces sweetened dates, chopped
1 cup crispy rice cereal
½ cup chopped pecans or walnuts
1 teaspoon vanilla
¾ cup powdered sugar

In a saucepan over medium-low heat, melt butter and honey together. Add dates and cook until dissolved, about 3 minutes. Remove from heat. Add cereal, nuts, and vanilla and mix until cereal is well coated. Allow to cool about 10 minutes. Scoop or form into 1" balls and roll in powdered sugar. Set aside to cool completely.

December 16
Good Elves Don't Stay on Shelves

Long before his counterpart on the shelf, my mom installed in our household the Elf on the Grandmother Clock. The grandmother clock in question was a generational heirloom handmade by a friend of the family from a tree on my great-grandparents' farm. I loved that old clock and could sit and stare at it all day, listening to its ticks and on-the-quarter-hour chimes…but not when the Elf was up on top.

According to Mom, this Elf was one of Santa's helpers. His job was to sit there day and night, night and day, observing our goings-on so he could report back on who would be making it onto the Nice List. Sure enough, when we woke up every Christmas Eve morning, the Elf would be gone from his perch without a trace. Our fate was sealed, and we'd be left to wonder until the next morning what the report would be.

Besides the inherently creepy nature of his job, there was always something about the Elf on the grandmother clock that bothered me. He was different from every other Elf I'd seen. Those elves were all so *busy*. There were Santa's Workshop elves, of course, always abuzz with making toys and preparing for their Christmas Eve deadline. We also saw mall and shopping center elves who collected gifts and donations to share with the poor, special assistance elves who helped people with disabilities to carry things and generally get around, and so many more. Elves were everywhere, and they were supposed to be *doing* something.

Even we took up the mantle as elves, at least for one day out of the season, and we definitely didn't just get to sit around. Instead, we delivered cookies on what Mom called our Santa Claus Route. The Santa Claus Route was an initiative Mom created during which we drove all over town from lunchtime until dark on the last weekend before Christmas and dropped off plates of goodies to our ministry leaders, shut-ins, and select family friends.

At first, Mandy and I were not big fans of the Santa Claus route because we were always the ones commissioned to go to the door. It was our job to knock, say "Merry Christmas!" as we handed the occupants their parcels, and become the unwilling recipients of their enthusiastic gratitude (this usually required hugging – not the favorite pastime of the introverts we were). The first time we asked why we had to do it, Mom said, "Santa Claus can't be expected to do everything, girls. He needs his elves to get out there and do some of the footwork. Now go put on your coats before I give you something real to complain about."

Upon reflection and maturing (at least a little, I hope), this is the best picture of the Church that I've ever heard. We are the hands and feet of God in this world. We are not Elves on shelves (or grandmother clocks), glibly hanging above others' heads, keeping score and vaguely or even directly threatening others with judgment. We are literally commissioned by Jesus Himself to get out there and love people by any means necessary.

I'm still an introvert, I probably still complain too much, and I still get creeped out by elves that perch instead of getting down to work. You have one job, Shelf Elf: make Christmas happen for someone who needs it. Stop staring at everyone and do something helpful.

You'll have much more fun, and we'll all be happier. Promise.

Questions for Discussion/Reflection:

1. Have you ever gotten to be an Elf at Christmas time? If so, what did you do in this role? How did you feel about it? If not, would you like to?

2. Read Matthew 2:9-11. The Magi travelled far to deliver their gifts to Jesus. Why do you think they chose the gifts they did? What do the gifts look like in your imagination?

3. In Mark 16:15, the risen Jesus commissions the disciples to "Go into all the world and proclaim the good news to the whole creation." What do you think the "good news" is? How does it relate to the "good news" He spoke of in Luke 4:18-19? What is one way you can be the bearer of good news to someone in your family or church this Christmas?

Pray For:

Retail Workers

Recipe of the Day: Cranberry Nut Bread

This bread is as beautiful as it is tasty – and it looks great wrapped on a plate, ready to share with someone who needs a pick-me-up!

> 2 cups + 1 tablespoon flour
> 1 cup sugar
> ½ teaspoon salt
> 1 ½ teaspoon baking powder
> ½ teaspoon baking soda
> 2 eggs
> ¾ cup orange juice
> 2 tablespoons sunflower oil
> 1 ½ cups fresh cranberries, chopped
> 1 cup chopped almonds

Preheat the oven to 350°F. Sift 2 cups flour, sugar, salt, baking powder, and baking soda together; set aside. Combine eggs, orange juice, and oil; add to the dry mixture. Toss cranberries and nuts together with 1 tablespoon of flour; add to the rest of the ingredients. Pour batter into a greased and floured loaf pan; bake for 60 minutes or until toothpick inserted in the center comes out clean. Cool in the pan for 10 minutes, then turn out onto a wire rack and cool completely.

It Takes a
Christmas Village

December 17
To Aunt Cindy's House We Go!

My mom has one birth sister, and we call her Aunt Cindy. Aunt Cindy was a little bit magical to us. She always knew what we were thinking (good or bad), always came up with the perfect outings (and could outlast our energy levels on any of them), and always gave us what we wanted (or explained to us why we actually wanted something else…and she was right!).

It follows, then, that Aunt Cindy's house was (and still is) one of our favorite places to go, because Aunt Cindy's house was different from ours in many magical ways.

At our house, we had to clean our plates every meal no matter what. At Aunt Cindy's house, we didn't even have to USE plates, and we only had to clean up our messes.

At our house, we had to go to bed at 8:00 sharp. At Aunt Cindy's house, we camped out in the living room and didn't go to sleep until we couldn't help it.

At our house, we had to eat our vegetables – usually green, oniony, and boiled into submission. At Aunt Cindy's house…what's a vegetable?

One year, when we still lived two states away, we got to visit Aunt Cindy's house for Christmas, and that was different, too. Instead of the roast beef dinner my mom made every year, we had Cornish game hens. Instead of our artificial Christmas tree with giant ceramic bulbs, we had a fresh-cut, fragrant blue spruce with white fairy lights. And instead of just putting out cookies and milk for Santa Claus on Christmas Eve, we also put out carrots.

That one was weird to me. Setting our tableau for Santa in front of the tree, I was fascinated by that bulbous, stringy bunch of carrots sitting to the side, trying desperately to figure out how they could belong. Were we trying to suggest that Santa needed to clean up his diet or what? Finally, when Aunt Cindy asked me to hand her the carrots, I couldn't hold back any more. "But what are they for?" I blurted.

"They're for the reindeer, of course," she answered brightly. "They're working awfully hard, helping Santa make all those deliveries. Don't you think they deserve a treat?"

Important note: I was about eight years old at this time, and rumors had been swirling at Warren G. Harding Elementary School that Santa Claus was not real. I didn't want to believe it, but I also didn't want to be the last one to know, just in case. Thus, when Aunt Cindy said this about the carrots, I was both thrilled and guarded. I probably said something intelligent like, "Cool" as I fanned the carrots out near the milk, and I resolved to wait and see what happened.

It turns out that Christmas morning at Aunt Cindy's house had several things in common with our own. There was the waking way too early, the dragging of adults out of bed, and the shooting like loosed arrows to the foot of the Christmas tree so we could explore the wonders beneath. The biggest difference was Santa's table.

Beside the plate of crumbs and dregs of milk I expected to find, there also sat exactly one nub of a carrot…with tooth marks in it.

I was amazed. I was flabbergasted. My hopes soared as my faith was validated. I had doubted because of the chatter about parents faking us kids out by eating Santa's treats, but this to me was proof positive of the opposite. No one in Aunt

Cindy's house even *liked* raw carrots! My faith had been given a magical boost.

I don't even remember what presents were under the tree for me that year. The best gift I got was a table scrap, and I didn't have doubts again for a very long time.

Questions for Discussion/Reflection:

1. Have you ever needed a boost in your faith walk? Have you ever had an opportunity to boost someone else's faith? What happened?

2. Read Luke 2:22-38. These two people had waited all their lives for proof that God would keep His promises to them. How do you think they held on to their faith for so long?

3. Read Hebrews 11:1. Look around you as you move through your day. What evidence of your faith do you see in this Christmas season?

Pray For:

People Who Need a Faith Boost

Recipe of the Day: Buttermilk Squares

Aunt Cindy will tell you that this is an old, traditional Southern recipe she found and she can't take any credit for it, but don't you believe it. There's magic in her spoon.

½ cup salted butter, melted
1 ½ cups sugar
3 eggs, room temperature and beaten
1 ½ tablespoons flour
1 teaspoon vanilla
½ cup buttermilk
1 pie crust (your favorite recipe or pre-made is fine)

Preheat oven to 400°F. Press pie crust into an ungreased 8" or 9" square pan (glass is best). Beat butter and sugar together until fluffy. Add the eggs and beat, then add vanilla. Alternate adding the flour with the buttermilk to the batter; beat until smooth. Pour into the pie crust and bake at 400° for 10 minutes, then reduce heat to 350° and bake for an additional 50-60 minutes (it is done when a golden-brown crust forms and a knife inserted in center comes out clean). Allow to cool completely before cutting into squares.

December 18
The Baby is Fine

My sister, Mandy was a sensitive soul growing up.

As the youngest in the family for several years, she bore unwanted attention for being little and cute long after she felt it to be a compliment. We cooed and took a million pictures every year of her in the church's nativity scene; she scowled and glowered from the stage because she was always cast as the donkey. We kept buying her soft and adorable pink clothes to go with her golden hair; she wanted to wear basketball shorts and t-shirts so she could play in the mud. But I think the worst of all these indignities was her penchant for clumsiness (a family characteristic) and our collective inability to stop thinking it was precious and hilarious.

It wasn't Mandy's fault. Between the ages of 12 and 15, she grew from about 5′3″ to her final adult height of 6′ even. She outgrew her shoes and clothes sizes at least every three months, and she could barely cross a room without creating a ten-foot swath of destruction in her wake…on a good day. By the time Aunt Cindy had our cousin Darcy, Mandy was beyond ready to stop being the baby and finally be grown up and respectable.

Darcy came along at just the right time for us. We were old enough to babysit but young enough to have the energy and availability to keep up with her. We tried to tuck her in our pockets and take her with us wherever we went. She was our mascot, our friend, and our baby.

And so it was that, as Aunt Cindy was preparing to depart from our house one evening, Mandy asked if she could carry Darcy to the car. There came an immediate hush over the room, and Aunt Cindy's silent side-eye conversation with Mom inadvertently spoke volumes. They were nervous.

Mandy picked up on the trepidation and was instantly enraged. "This is so unfair! Why doesn't anyone ever trust me with anything? Just because I broke the punch bowl last week and my toe on the bathtub over the summer doesn't mean I would actually hurt The Baby. Jeez!" The tirade went on much longer than that, but you get the idea.

She was right, really. Words are powerful and what you speak over a person has a way of seeping in and becoming self-fulfilling prophecy. Properly chagrined (and confident that Darcy's 14 layers of clothes plus her fleece-lined and down-padded snowsuit would have rendered her unbreakable anyway), Aunt Cindy acquiesced and shouldered the diaper bag as Mandy led out the front door with The Baby in tow.

Anger lingers, and teenage anger smolders the longest, which is why what happened next became the stuff of family legend to this day. All the way down the hill that comprised our driveway, Mandy sounded something like this: "Nobody ever believes me, Darcy. I hope you're never a clumsy kid like me, I tell you that. One broken lamp and they'll hide all the china from you forever. What is it going to take for me to finally get a little – *Aaah!*" This was followed by a whisper of a swishing sound and then a mild thump.

From my position at our front door, it was hard to make out exactly what had happened, due partly to the darkness of the evening and partly to Mom's and Aunt Cindy's obscuring my view, doubled over and helpless with laughter. I dashed past them with what I'm told was a fiercely reproving glare, down the steps to find Mandy lying flat on her back in the driveway and securely holding Darcy aloft as though playing a game of

Super Baby. All the while, she was calling out loudly and in a most disgusted tone, "The Baby is fine. The Baby is FINE." As if to back her up, Darcy was cooing and smiling and perfectly entertained. She would have been happy to do it again.

I held The Baby for Mandy as she righted herself and checked for damage. There was none to Darcy or to her...unless you factor in the years to come of recounting this story to as many people as will listen as often as we can find occasion to tell it, from that day to this one and probably beyond.

Questions for Discussion/Reflection:

1. Have you ever had a reputation for something you didn't particularly like or agree with? How did you handle it? Have you ever been the one speaking negatively about someone else?

2. Read Matthew 1:18-19. Joseph was prepared to go to great lengths to protect Mary's dignity. Why do you think that is, when, as far as he knew, he had every right to shame her publicly?

3. Proverbs 18:21 tells us, "The tongue has the power of life and death." What does that mean? How can you use your power for life and for good this Christmas?

Pray For:

Teenagers

Recipe of the Day: Snickerdoodles

These cookies are the favorites of our now-grown cousin Darcy, who managed to develop into a perfectly balanced and healthy woman, despite all our influence and efforts.

> 1 cup salted butter, softened
> 1 ½ cups sugar
> 2 eggs
> 2 ¾ cups flour
> 2 teaspoons cream of tartar
> 1 teaspoon baking soda
> ¼ cup sugar + 2 teaspoons ground cinnamon, mixed

Preheat oven to 350°F. Cream butter and sugar until light and fluffy. Add egg; mix well. Sift flour, cream of tartar, and baking soda together; add to creamed mixture gradually until thoroughly blended. Roll or scoop dough into 2" balls and roll in a bowl of the cinnamon-sugar mixture to coat. Place on ungreased cookie sheets about 3" apart. Bake for 7-9 minutes or until bottom edges are just beginning to brown. Cool for 2-3 minutes on cookie sheets, then transfer to a cooling rack to cool completely.

December 19
Fireworks in the Rain

Growing up without a father in the home is hard, to be sure, but it's a lot harder on most families than it was for us because Aunt Cindy had the good sense (and/or wildly fantastic fortune) to marry my Uncle Marc. If I had to sum up Uncle Marc in one word, it would be *present*. He is always paying attention, always appreciating, and always there for you.

Mention offhandedly that your toilet is acting up? Uncle Marc shows up for the next visit with his toolbox in hand. Pull into their driveway with a broken tail light or low tires? When you come back out after lunch, it will be mysteriously fixed. My favorite was the time I slept over and Aunt Cindy asked me to help her remember to bring lip balm the next day; in the morning, both of us having utterly forgotten that lip balm even existed, we found a fresh tube of it sitting in the seat of her car.

Even when he's not there, he's there. Uncle Marc has worked as a cross-country truck driver for many, many years (which keeps him on the road except for on weekends and the biggest holidays), but we always know he's thinking about us. He brings home souvenirs, sends money for us to use for school clothes and other necessities, and even saves all his quarters in case there's a missing one from our National Parks quarters collection in there somewhere.

Fireworks with Uncle Marc began one Fourth of July when he surprised us with a variety pack he'd picked up on the spur of the moment. Uncle Marc's boyish delight in setting them off created an unparalleled accidental comedy routine. If it was a good one, he'd jump and yell as much as any kid present. If it was a dud, he'd unleash a barrage of dry, sardonic insults at it and drop-kick its smoky remains into the fire pit. Best of all was when one would veer off course – almost always directly toward him – and he'd yelp and scamper about like a jackrabbit. He never actually got hurt, he's far too fast and graceful for that, but he put on a show better than any fairgrounds or waterfront or televised event.

Unfortunately, the world of driving and logistics is no respecter of family traditions. Uncle Marc is not always able to make it back exactly on the Fourth of July, but we always insist on waiting to do fireworks with him. Some years we only run a few weeks late, some it's more like months, but no matter how long it takes, we always keep the bin of fireworks safe, dry, and put away until we can all enjoy them together.

We've had Fourth of July fireworks on the fifth of July, Labor Day, the middle of October, and even New Year's Eve. That one was my favorite because, as the night wore on, a mist of rain began to descend over the yard. By the time we had our traditional closing sparklers, the smoke and water droplets had combined to create a magical, multi-colored fog over us all. Happy New Year, indeed!

The most important thing a girl like me ever needed from a male role model was the keeping of promises, and that's what Uncle Marc has given me. Fireworks don't always come when I expect or schedule or want them, but I never doubt they will happen. And when they do, rain or shine, they will be better than any substitute the entire rest of the world could have offered.

Questions for Discussion/Reflection:

1. Do you always keep your promises? Do people always keep their promises to you? What do you think it is that makes promises difficult to keep sometimes?

2. Read Matthew 8:17, 12:17-21, and 21:4-5. Why do you think the writer of Matthew kept reminding us of these prophecies when telling Jesus's story?

3. Remember that in Isaiah 41:10, God promises us, "I will strengthen you and help you; I will uphold you with my righteous right hand." Do you ever struggle to believe this or any of God's promises? How can the Christmas story help you to grow in trusting God this season?

Pray For:

Children of Absent Parents

Recipe of the Day: Pineapple Cookies

These cookies were Mom's gift to Uncle Marc at least once a year in thanks for all the help he gave us with repairs and such. If his reaction was any indicator, they were more than sufficient.

½ cup salted butter, softened
1 cup sugar
1 egg
1 teaspoon vanilla
8-ounce can crushed pineapple, drained (reserve juice for glaze)
2 cups flour
1 ½ teaspoons baking powder
¼ teaspoon baking soda
pineapple glaze frosting (1 cup powdered sugar + 1-2 teaspoons pineapple juice)

Preheat oven to 350°F. Cream butter and sugar until light and fluffy. Add egg, pineapple, and vanilla; mix well. Sift dry ingredients together; add to creamed mixture gradually until thoroughly blended (may need to add flour if dough is too sticky to roll). Roll or scoop dough into 2" balls and place on greased cookie sheets about 2" apart. Cover the closed end of a glass with a damp baking towel and press each cookie gently to flatten it (but not too flat, or cookies will crumble). Bake for 7-9 minutes or until bottom edges are just beginning to brown. Cool for 2-3 minutes on cookie sheets, then transfer to a wire rack to cool completely. When completely cooled, brush with glaze and allow to set.

December 20
Choosy Moms' Best Friends Choose Jif®

There's the family you love and the family you choose and if you're lucky, there's also the family that chooses you. By far the most regular Chosen Family presence in our home and our life was my mom's best friend, whom we lovingly dubbed Aunt Connie.

Aunt Connie was a fiery woman, gifted at genius levels with both music and humor. She knew everyone in the Christian music industry (or so it seemed to me), and she had a love of animals greater than anyone I've ever known save for perhaps my own children. She and Mom were legends at the local Denny's for their regularly scheduled nights of coffee and conversation that would extend into the wee morning hours.

I used to hope I would have someone like Aunt Connie in my life when I was grown-up like Mom. What I know now but didn't fully realize at the time is that Aunt Connie was already my friend, too. She didn't think of or treat me as just her best friend's kid; she supported me and invested in me and was there for me whenever I needed or wanted her.

One way this showed up was in the annual gift of the peanut butter. I don't remember exactly how or why it came up, but during our gift planning one year, Mandy and I asked what Aunt Connie would like. Mom (herself being an amazing best friend and not wishing to unload on Aunt Connie with knick-knacks or odd fundraiser items) suggested practically, "I don't know, she's a big fan of peanut butter."

Peanut butter? Really?

"Oh yes, it's her absolute favorite thing. I've seen her sit and eat Jif® Extra Crunchy peanut butter right out of the jar with a spoon!"

Well, that settled it. Nothing would do the next time we were at the store but that we should get the biggest jar of Jif® Extra Crunchy peanut butter we could find. We wrapped it to the best of our ability, topped it with the biggest green Christmas bow we could find, and put it under the tree.

The look on Aunt Connie's face when she opened that gift was everything. She gave Mom a quick glance (which Mom returned with a smile and a shrug), and threw her head back with laughter. Eyes dancing, she declared that she LOVED it, this was her favorite tasty treat in the world. Then with a snap of her fingers, she intoned in a flawless French accent, "But I must have zee spoon! Where is zee spoon so that I may savor my tasty treat?"

Mandy and I raced to the kitchen and stumbled over each other like a herd of puppies to answer this summons. Then, spoon firmly in hand, Aunt Connie removed the seal and took two huge bites of her peanut butter – right out of the jar, just as the legend described! We were astonished at her freedom and hedonism, but also delighted and wriggly with glee.

What Aunt Connie *didn't* do is every bit as important as what she did. She didn't patronize or humor us. She didn't belittle us or see us as less than anyone else in the room. Aunt Connie looked into the heart of our gift and saw that it was our best for her; she would respond with nothing but her best in return. Our gift, and we ourselves, were truly seen and valued.

The very next year – as if they somehow knew – Jif® came out with their Extra Crunchy peanut butter in a four-pound size.

Questions for Discussion/Reflection:

1. What's the most thoughtful gift anyone ever gave you? What's the most thought you ever put into a gift for someone else? How was it received?

2. Read Matthew 19:13-15. Why do you think the disciples rebuked the children and their parents in the first place? What do you think Jesus's blessing meant to the ones who received it?

3. In Matthew 18:3, Jesus said, "Unless you change and become like little children, you will never enter the kingdom of heaven." What do you think he meant by that? How can you be more like a child this Christmas?

Pray For: Teachers and Children's Ministers

Recipe of the Day: Peanut Butter Crispy Treats
The next best thing to spooning it from a jar!

> 1 cup honey
> ¾ cup sugar
> 1 teaspoon vanilla
> 1 cup peanut butter (smooth or extra crunchy)
> 6 cups crispy rice cereal

In a saucepan over medium heat, cook honey and sugar until boiling. Remove from heat. Add vanilla and peanut butter and stir until well blended. Add cereal; mix until well coated. Spoon into a buttered 9"x13" pan and allow to cool about 20 minutes. Cut into bars, then let cool completely.

December 21
Blue Christmas

"I think there must be something wrong with me, Linus. Christmas is coming, but I'm not happy. I don't feel the way I'm supposed to feel..." –Charlie Brown[2]

I hate to admit this, but in the past, I have written off this bewildered confession as evidence of weak character on good old Charlie Brown's part. How can anyone not be happy at Christmas? There are lights and parties and movies and treats and friends and snow and presents... Why, you couldn't escape Christmas cheer if you tried, I'd have thought. Clearly, this was just a means to a story – almost an unbelievable stretch, to be honest.

Cut to me sitting in the living room at the end of one of our last Christmas Open Houses. It was a perfect holiday moment. I was quietly basking in the glow of the Christmas lights and the fireplace. My family had just said farewell to the last of our dozens of guests. Candles were burning, my tummy was full of homemade treats, and the house had settled into an almost poetic stillness. It was even gray and snowing outside, my personal favorite weather pattern. All was right with the world.

At least, it should have been. Yet even in the beauty and tranquility all around me, I could feel...nothing at all. I wasn't sad. I wasn't lonely or stressed out or fearful. I just could not connect with my surroundings and all that they should have imparted. *I don't feel the way I'm supposed to feel...* I get it now.

---

[2] Mendelson, Lee, Charles M. Schulz, Bill Melendez, Vince Guaraldi, Robert T. Gillis, David Benoit, Chuck McCann, et al. 2008. *A Charlie Brown Christmas*. Burbank, Calif: Warner Home Video.

Our media outlets work hard every year to paint us a picture of just how our holidays should look. The grocer's commercial assumes our typical families will be frolicking about the kitchen together. Morning radio shows inform us which toys and electronics are every happy kid's must-haves. Jewelers' billboards demonstrate the ideal couple's celebration, which is backlit by the frosty glow of a skating pond and features a diamond no smaller than your average beagle. These are the messages we constantly receive.

It's no doubt due to all of this helpful guidance that Christmas has a reputation for inciting depression. I mean, my family's baking projects may involve dancing, but most likely in an effort to extinguish spontaneously combusting butter or to peel the youngest child from the refrigerator's ledge. My parents' divorce was final years ago (probably due to a glaring lack of ice), and the economy continues to make a mockery of must-haves for anyone. It becomes easy to wilt under these messages of inadequacy and failure.

Thankfully, Isaiah 42:3 tells us: "A bruised reed [God] will not break, and a smoldering wick He will not snuff out." Whether the root of our blues is circumstantial, psychological, or biological, we can cling to this promise: God will not let us be extinguished completely. Above all things, Christmas is our reminder that God keeps His promises. He remembers us, and He will preserve us.

My new church has a tradition that is near and dear to my heart. In the middle of December, we hold a Blue Christmas (also sometimes called the Longest Night) service designed to address coping with the feelings of loss and depression that are so common this time of year. Basically, it provides an organized setting in which people have permission to feel whatever they need to feel, and to receive grace and prayer for it. I attend every year, sometimes to help and sometimes to be the one receiving help. Either way, I always leave with a sense of profound gratitude.

If you are among the blue this season, I encourage you to find a similar outlet if you can. You are not alone, nor are you defective. You have a good reason for feeling – or not – the way you do. I will be praying that you find resolution and relief, and that your flame will be rekindled.

If you are not one of us, then I simply implore you to be kind. We'll try not to cry all over your party clothes.

Questions for Discussion/Reflection:

1. What do you do when you feel sad? When you feel happy? When you feel bored? When you feel nothing at all?

2. Jesus talked about going through hard times in the Sermon on the Mount. Read Matthew 5:4. What does this promise mean to you?

3. Now read Psalm 43:5. What did the Psalmist decide to do to overcome his downcast soul/feelings?

Pray For:

People with Anxiety, Depression, and Other Mental Health Concerns

Recipe of the Day: Ice Cream Milk

Of course, your blues could also be a case of good old-fashioned seasonal affective disorder. If you can, I recommend going for a walk in the sun, then cozying up with your favorite dunking cookie and a tall glass (or mug, it's also great warm!) of this stuff right here.

> 8 ounces your milk of choice
> 1 teaspoon vanilla
> 1-3 tablespoons sugar (according to your desired sweetness)

Mix well and enjoy!

December 22
Miracle on Kennedy Avenue

When people think of Christmas dinner in America, they often picture turkey and all the fixin's. Depending on what part of the world your family is from, you may see a Christmas goose, roast suckling pig, oyster stew, or a Chinese food buffet. As for me personally, I always see chocolate milk. Here's why.

My grandfather came to visit us one Christmas from Seymour, Indiana, and my family decided to meet him for dinner at the Hessville Restaurant, one of our favorite haunts. What a scene we must have made for the staff on that day! I'm sure we took up about 75% of the floorplan and tables with our party of seven people plus outerwear and an entire sleigh's worth of presents…and so much noise and laughter! It was gray and blisteringly cold beyond the windows, but inside was all excitement and frivolity and warm, incandescent light.

I got to sit by Grandpa, which suited me just fine. He told stories, made everyone laugh, and pinched me every once in a while to make sure I knew he was paying attention. We didn't make it down to see him nearly often enough for our tastes, and not just because he and Grandma Dottie always had stockpiles of presents waiting for us. Grandpa is strong, hyper-intelligent, and the funniest human I've ever known. I did then, and always do now, feel smarter and happier just for spending time with him.

There I was, about halfway through the ridiculously extravagant array of French fries, tacos, and waffles he'd encouraged me to order, and my chocolate milk was nearly dry. I was taking small sips at this point, trying to make it last as long as possible because if history was any indicator, Mom would make me drink water after that. But when our server came by to refill Grandpa's coffee and to laugh at his jokes for the hundredth time, he asked her if she could also please bring me another chocolate milk.

ANOTHER chocolate milk. I looked to my mom, scared she'd make him take it back, but she just smiled and carried on her conversation. That made two things that had never happened to me up to this point: Mom's being overruled, and my getting extra drinks at a restaurant …then he ordered us dessert and hot chocolate, too!

Looking at his own plate, I noticed Grandpa had only ordered a plain grilled chicken, which didn't seem to fit with the rest of the bounty before us. When I asked him why that was all he got, he chuckled and told me in his deep, rumbling voice, "I don't know, I'm just a plain chicken kind of guy, I guess."

That was the day I became aware of Grandpa's gift of generosity and sharing. He gave us a Christmas meal never to be forgotten, and piles of presents to go with it. He gave our server about a 200% tip (and a near-fatal heart attack when she found it on the table, I'm sure). He gave the man on the corner with a cardboard sign a few bills from his wallet. Grandpa had worked hard all his life to get to a place of financial security, but keeping it to himself was never the plan. He earned so he could give, and generously at that. If I have one ambition in life as an adult, it's to be able to love and share and give as generously as my Grandpa without a care for my own comfort or any return.

Also, to buy as many chocolate milks as they can handle for as many children in my life as want them.

Questions for Discussion/Reflection:

1. What role does money play in your day-to-day life? Does it represent more of a blessing or more of a challenge?

2. Read James 1:17. How do you think this verse applies to the Christmas story? How does it apply to you personally?

3. In Matthew 6:20, Jesus tells us to "store up for yourselves treasures in heaven." What kinds of treasures are those? How might God be calling you to fill your heavenly treasure chest this Christmas?

Pray For:

The Homeless

Recipe of the Day: Candy Cane Coffee Cake

This was the Christmas treat we gave away more than any other each year, and Mom's friends were always delighted to see it coming.

1 package active dry yeast
¼ cup lukewarm water
¼ cup (½ stick) salted butter, melted
¼ cup sugar
¾ cup water
1/3 cup instant dry milk
1 egg
3 ½ cups sifted flour

Filling: ¾ cup walnuts
strawberry preserves

Dissolve yeast in water. Combine with butter, sugar, water, dry milk, and egg. Gradually add flour and mix well. Turn dough onto lightly floured surface; knead until smooth and elastic. Place in a greased bowl and turn to coat all sides. Cover and allow to rise in a warm place until doubled in size. Punch down and divide into 3 parts; let sit 10 minutes. As you wait, combine the preserves and nuts.

Roll one dough portion into a rectangle about 15"x6". Make cuts along the long sides about 1" apart and 2" deep. Spread 1/3 of the nut mixture down the center of the dough. Alternately fold dough strips over the filling; place onto a lightly greased cookie sheet and shape into a candy cane/hook. Cover and let rise until doubled in size. Repeat with the other two dough portions.

Preheat oven to 350°F. Bake 12-15 minutes or until golden brown. Decorate with frosting or glaze and red decorating sugar, if desired.

December 23
The Kingdom for a Cookie

The most beautiful Christmas tree I ever saw was a discard on its way to the dump.

It had been a lean Christmas for us, and in the absence of more elaborate decorations, my mother built a simple faux fireplace on the main wall of our living room. The mantel allowed just enough room for my stocking and for the nativity scene to rest in prominent view as the center of our celebration. The whole display was made of cardboard, but it was colorful and festive and she got it special for me, so it was perfect for us.

My mom's brother, Uncle Chip, who came visiting the day after Christmas, found it confusing. He pressed my mother at some length for a good reason that I did not have a Christmas tree, as all children rightfully should. (This is probably a good time to note that it was my first Christmas, and he was only five years old.) Not having the financial acumen or social sensitivity required to grasp the situation, he finally resigned himself to the injustice of it all and – no doubt at the vigorous behest of the adults – decided to spend his energies playing outside.

Some time later, in the midst of dinner preparations, my uncle came bursting back into the house. He was red-faced and out of breath, yet oddly reserved and mannerly for a young boy in the throes of vigorous exercise. This could mean only one thing: he wanted something.

Sure enough, not even waiting for a pause in the conversation, Uncle Chip donned his most cherubic face and inquired as to whether he might have six of my mother's chocolate chip cookies, please, right away. This was oddly specific. My mother had made plenty of cookies and was happy to dispense them to her sweet little brother generously, but there was something curious in his manner that led her to question him. Why six cookies, and why the urgency?

It turns out, my uncle hadn't resigned himself to injustice at all; he had been busily setting things right. As he was enjoying the outdoors, one of our neighbor boys had been assigned the chore of taking his family's used Christmas tree to the curb for pickup. Sensing providence and opportunity, my uncle immediately approached the boy and began wheeling and dealing for its acquisition. Since cookies were the only currency available to him, that's what he offered and the neighbor decided six would be fair. All my uncle needed was to take those cookies out, and the tree would be ours.

Swallowing back a rising lump in her throat, my mother opened the cookie jar and let him choose his six perfect cookies. He ran them outside, then talked his new friend into helping to carry the tree into our house. These two earnest young boys muscled my tree across the street, through the door, and into a corner near the nativity scene, somehow managing to prop it up securely enough for display.

This was some tree. Its original perfect form was now lopsided from the weight of its former decorations. There were scattered clumps of crushed icicles all over it on random branches. It had lost a fair number of needles at the hands of its young movers, too – but it was mine: my tree, my gift, bought with the uninhibited love of a young boy who cared enough to go find it for me. Love made it perfect.

I don't know whether my family added any decorations to my tree that night, or how long it was allowed to stay. In truth, I don't actually have a visual memory of it at all, just images imprinted on my heart from the story as we've told it over the years. Yet that tattered old leftover tree remains as the standard to which I hold all Christmas trees, and the epitome of love made tangible and real.

Oh, and to this day, my mother still gives her little brother cookies for Christmas. Every year.

Questions for Discussion/Reflection:

1. Have you ever given or received a gift that was actually something old (an antique, a family heirloom, etc.)? How did you feel about it? Was it more or less valuable for being something old?

2. Read John 1:1-4. Jesus was with God from the beginning, but when He came to earth as a baby, He was brand new to us! How do these words inform and/or affect your view of the nativity scene?

3. 2 Corinthians 5:17 says, "If anyone is in Christ, the new creation has come: The old has gone, the new is here!" How does Jesus make us new? Is there something in your home you can repurpose into a new creation as a symbol of new life in Jesus this Christmas?

Pray For:

People Who Need a New Beginning

Recipe of the Day: Tribley Bars

These are cookies that Mom makes for Uncle Chip every year. They never get old for him.

8-ounce package dates, chopped (about 1 ½ cups)
1 cup packed brown sugar
1 cup water

¾ cup salted butter, melted
1 cup packed brown sugar
1 ½ cups flour
1 ¾ cup quick oats
1 tablespoon baking powder

Preheat oven to 325°F. In saucepan over medium heat, cook dates, brown sugar, and water until dissolved and thick. Combine the remaining ingredients until crumbly. Press about 2/3 of the crust mixture into the bottom and halfway up the sides of a 9"x13" pan. Once date mixture has cooled completely, pour on top of crust and spread evenly. Cover with the rest of the crust mixture. Bake for 30 minutes or until set and very lightly browned. Allow to cool completely before slicing into bars.

December 24
Lights in the Sky

Most churches offer some kind of a Christmas Eve service, but few put on a true Midnight Mass, which just happens to be my mom's favorite service of the year. The tradition started many hundreds of years ago when Christians began to hold vigils in preparation for important feasts, Christmas being among them. It is so named because the truest form of the service would begin at midnight, but Mom much prefers the ones that begin at 11:00 and end as Christmas Day is ringing in.

One thing I love about my mom is, if her church doesn't offer a particular observance that she loves, she will simply find another church to visit for the occasion. Growing up, we went to Lutheran churches for Good Friday services, Messianic Jewish gatherings for Seder meals, and Methodist chapels for Longest Night readings. I learned early on to be comfortable as a visitor and to see the value in learning diverse methods of practicing our faith.

The first Christmas Eve Midnight Mass I remember attending felt simultaneously solemn, jubilant, and indulgent. First of all, we got to stay up late to attend (which meant an extra pass at the cookie jar after bedtime to help us stay awake). Since we were visitors in another congregation, we also got to put on our very best Sunday clothes and shiniest shoes. It kind of felt like we were going to a late-night party with the grown-ups.

Most of the rest of what I remember is just images and impressions. I knew all of the songs because they were traditional Christmas hymns. The sermon went a little long for my personal tastes (as did they all for me at that time), but I knew the passage from Luke 2 by heart (thank you, *A Charlie*

Brown Christmas!). I was warm and sleepy, calm and comfortable within this new place and experience.

The part I remember most clearly was the candle-lighting ceremony. When we first entered the sanctuary, we were each given one of those small white candles with the paper discs around the middle. Near the end of the service, the pastor said a few words, then lit his candle from one on the altar. He used his to light the candles of two ushers, then they went into the congregation and began passing the light to the people at the ends of each pew. Within minutes, the entire body of believers was alight as we sang, "Silent Night" in unison.

Standing in the light of all those candles and our glowing faces that Christmas Eve, I felt for the first time what it meant to be one with the body of believers. With our candles held near chest level, we all looked pretty much the same – our differences smoothed out and blended together in the warm, amber glow of the candles. Our individual flames came together to make one giant light that limned the room so all could see.

On the way home that night, I was transfixed by the light of the stars burning outside my car window. I couldn't help but think that if they weren't so far apart, the stars could light the earth more effectively. If all those stars could come together into one big light in the middle, no shadow on earth could escape their shine.

They'd be just like the sun.

Questions for Discussion/Reflection:

1. What is it that stands out to you when it's dark outside? Do you have a favorite constellation or star? A favorite night sky feature?

2. Read Matthew 2:10. The star was the Magi's sign that they were in the right place at the right time, that they had succeeded in their mission. How did they celebrate? How do you celebrate success?

3. Philippians 2:15 encourages us to shine "like stars in the sky." What does that mean to you? How can you shine with other believers this Christmas?

Pray For:

Unity among Believers

Recipe of the Day: Pound Cake

This cake was the centerpiece of our Christmas dessert table every year. If we were very good, we might even get to break into it before going to bed after Midnight Mass!

> 1 cup (2 sticks) salted butter
> 1 ¾ cups sugar
> 5 eggs, slightly beaten
> 2 cups flour
> ½ teaspoon lemon extract
> ½ teaspoon vanilla
> yellow food coloring to taste
>
> Glaze: 1 cup sugar
> ½ cup water

Preheat oven to 350°F. Cream butter and sugar until fluffy. Alternate adding eggs and flour until well combined. Stir in remaining ingredients and mix well. Pour batter into a greased and floured tube pan and bake for 55 minutes or until toothpick inserted in center comes out clean. Just before the cake is done, heat glaze ingredients to boiling; pour over hot cake immediately after removing it from the oven. Cool completely before removing from pan.

Bonus
Here's Mud in your Eye!

'Twas the night after Christmas…and Mom dragged us to church.

It's not that I had any particular problem with going to church or anything. Church was always a happy place where I felt noticed and affirmed and at peace. There was VBS, Sunday School, lots of hugs, and even doughnuts sometimes. What's not to like?

But this was December 26th. Even at the robust and indefatigable age of six years old, I was tired. We had successfully pulled off another Christmas Open House plus miscellaneous other entertainments, family get-togethers, Santa Claus routes, school performances and plays, special church services, and who-knows-what else. I was ready for the celebrating to be done.

Mom was not having it. Aunt Connie's Cousin Jimmy would be visiting our church that night to do a special concert and we were going no matter what. If Jesus Himself had returned before that concert was over, I truly believe Mom would have greeted Him with a polite hug, then invited Him to sit by her and finish the concert before she'd go anywhere.

So off to church we went, and later on, I'd be happy we did.

Cousin Jimmy had me from his first note because he was performing the entire concert on a stool with an acoustic guitar. That was an extreme novelty in our church at that time (it was a conservative assembly which barely even allowed organ music). He was also a skilled storyteller who could weave songs along with Bible passages and testimonies into a lovely tapestry of color and sound.

Very near the end of his set, Cousin Jimmy told the story of the blind beggar whom Jesus healed by applying a paste of earth and His own spit onto the man's eyes. I'd heard the story before, could probably even have told it myself, but something new in me clicked into place at that moment. For the first time, I saw more in the story than just a Sunday School lesson; I could see Jesus's heart for the world and more specifically, for me personally. Jesus wanted to help people. Jesus wanted suffering to end. Jesus wanted us all not just to exist, but to live and to SEE.

I didn't completely notice I was crying until Mom put her hand on me and leaned down to whisper, "Are you okay?"

I nodded. And I knew what I had to do. I told her I wanted to go up front where I'd seen so many other people go before. I wanted to be baptized.

When the time came and the pastor stood up front, we stepped from our pew out into the aisle. I clasped my mother's hand and began to step forward, but she didn't move. When I looked back to see what was wrong, she leaned down and let my hand go. She said, "I'm sorry, Sweetie, but I can't hold your hand right now. If you know this is something you want to do, you need to walk to the front freely on your own. This is special between you and God, and it's with Him that you should walk right now."

I didn't love this turn of events, but I kind of sensed what she meant. I took a deep breath, steeled my nerves, and walked what suddenly felt like about a mile and a half to the pastor. As the congregation sang, he asked me why I was there and I told him. He smiled, put his hand on my back, and turned me around so he could present me to the people when the song was over.

And do you know what I saw when I turned around? My mom, the woman who gave me life and spent nearly all of her time and energy trying to uphold it, was standing right behind me the whole time.

Questions for Discussion/Reflection:

1. What's your favorite Jesus story? When did you first know there was something special about Him?

2. Read John 9:1-7. What do you think it was like to see for the very first time, having lived for so many years in blindness?

3. In Luke 4:18, Jesus said, "[God] has anointed me to proclaim good news to the poor. He has sent me to proclaim freedom for the prisoners and recovery of sight for the blind, to set the oppressed free…" How may your sight need to be recovered or refreshed this Christmas?

Pray For:

People Who Are Blind Physically and Spiritually

Recipe of the Day: Happy Birthday, Jesus! Cake

Later, when I had my own children and we instituted a tradition of cake and ice cream for Jesus's birthday, we took a vote on which cake recipe to use. This won by a landslide.

½ cup salted butter, softened
1 ½ cups sugar
2 eggs
1 teaspoon vanilla
1-ounce bottle red food coloring
1 cup buttermilk
1 teaspoon vinegar
I teaspoon baking soda
2 teaspoons cocoa
2 ¼ cups flour

Preheat oven to 350°F. Cream butter and sugar until light and fluffy. Add eggs, vanilla, food coloring, and buttermilk; mix well. Add vinegar and baking soda, allowing them to fizz together for 1 minute before stirring in. Sift cocoa and flour together; add to creamed mixture gradually and mix with electric mixer for 2 minutes. Pour into three 8" or 9" cake pans and bake for 20 minutes or until toothpick inserted in the center comes out clean. Allow to cool completely.

When cool, layer your cake with frosting of your choice. We use the one on the next page.

Peppermint Cream Cheese Frosting

     1 cup salted butter, softened
     2 packages cream cheese, 8-ounces each
     1 teaspoon vanilla
     1 teaspoon peppermint extract
     a splash of heavy cream
     2 cups powdered sugar

Mix until smooth, adding the powdered sugar last and gradually.

Index of Recipes

34873276R00069

Made in the USA
Columbia, SC
18 November 2018